"I Wasn't Kidding, Now, I AM"

"I Wasn't Kidding, Now, I AM"

Family Matters, Confidence Builders plus 101 other activities for children ages FOUR to TEN that also keep parents sane & involved. Effective & Fun

Part 1

By Rory J. Hill

Paperback ISBN: 979-8988640707
Hardcover ISBN: 979-8988640721

"Those who have children can become masters of patience, endurance, & steadfastness, because children will test you at every turn" The way to make our children patient & loving is to be that way ourselves"

Eknath Easwaran

"The greatest gift we can give children, is the appreciation of their uniqueness"

Fred Rodgers (Aka - Mr. Rodgers)

I know what it is to be your age
You don't know what it's like to be mine

My Dad (Melvin Hill)

"There is a big difference between being "Childlike & Childish"
May you always enjoy the wonder of being "Childlike."

Me, Rory J. Hill

DEDICATION:

"I Wasn't Kidding, Now, I Am" is dedicated to **ALL PARENTS** who work hard to create the best foundation & opportunities for their children

ACKNOWLEDGEMENTS

"I Wasn't Kidding, Now, I Am" was inspired by successful role models who helped me notice & appreciate the wonderment & uniqueness of the relationship & bond between parents & their children.

Julie, a mom totally dedicated to her kids. She is not only dedicated to their growth but also to their childhood & to their laughter. I began authoring this book in 2006.

Julie's daughters Kylie & Emma (now 25 & 27) who served as "kid" test subjects They gave me the good the bad & the ugly from their "kid" point of view. Thank you for playing! You have given me much joy & laughter while creating this book.

Dad, Melvin Hill for being a big man in many different ways. He never was afraid to bring emotion & humor into every day.

Mom, Marjorie Hill for helping me to be more aware of the simple things in life, music, laughter & imagination.

Brother Brian, who always listened when I got stuck & for always being there for me.

Sister Tammy Johnson, an unstoppable mom, good friend & little sister. She always uses love, laughter & a great deal of patience to teach her three wonderful children. I also thank you for letting me use your kids as the original "test" kids.

JoAnn for all the things she helped me do when I was less than motivated, helped me to move forward & not to be held back by trying to be perfect. Results, progress, laughter & love got me to the finish

Finally, thanks to those unnamed parents who don't even know that you helped me by letting me babysit your children over 40 years ago!

I hope they turned out ok.

TABLE OF CONTENTS:

HISTORY:

Why write this book? It's just "Elementary"

Because kids are unique gifts, perfect at birth

They need & deserve all the love, nurturing & guidance possible

They are our greatest hope for the future

To help parents to provide a strong family foundation, establish boundaries

To allow their child(ren) to develop their natural abilities.

To guide & sometimes to discipline with love

To add safety to their day & yours

Why this age group? FOUR to TEN

They are old enough to understand & perform while young enough to still be malleable & receptive to **"Foundation Building"** There are 28 million of them according to the 2022 Census

To keep a bit of a kid in all of us!

Why me? This book called me to write it.

It called me because you see, I don't have children. Although I love kids, the stars never lined up for me to have any of my own. Maybe, that's what made me so aware of kids in general.

As long as I can remember, I have questioned why some kids get ahead & are happy while others get into trouble. Some are blocked by shyness & some by lack of direction or boundaries. I wondered if that could be changed.

I avoided trouble as a kid but suffered from both shyness & lack of direction. I (now) realize that my parents did the best they could. I love them, yet they lacked the ability to nurture my "uniqueness." This lack of nurturing took many years to overcome on my own.

I've always had a sense of fairness (my Libra way). I want all kids to have a fair chance. From the time I was eighteen, I began interacting with little kids & I connected with them through volunteering. I treated them all as being unique & with respect. I paid attention to them.

They in return shared many amazing **"kid sights"** - the ways a kid looks at things" with me. They always responded to the many activities I created to connect with them. They used a language they could understand. Their honesty showed me what was needed & appreciated to connect with them.

I also listened while moms talked about their challenges of raising kids (many as single moms). Many of their struggles included "how to be good moms while working in or outside the home."

They constantly agonized about missing the experiences of their kids' childhood. They told me that they were looking for ways to counter the "outside" influences which impact their children. Those influences were not always in line with their family values.

A market opportunity also spoke to me. I searched for diverse books, courses or coaching (seminars, tapes or CDs) anything that helped parents build a child's emotional muscle. Muscle to maintain their personal family values as parents told them that's what "they" believed.

I researched & researched but there was not anything to touch the many angles of child rearing from the kid's point of view or addressed these parent goals. I decided to take on the challenge of developing them myself!

I hope you have as much fun using these activities with your children as I have with creating them. They have all been **kid/parent tested** for fun & effectiveness. I know you too will have the success that others have enjoyed.

Children really are our future. I, for one, do not want to imagine the future without the ideas that begin with a creative & confident child.

NEEDS ANALYSIS:

Is this book for them & you?

Do you still have some kid inside of you? Then you want this book

Do you have some of these **Characteristics of a Child**? Then you want this book

Characteristics of a Child

Seek out things that are fun to do

Jump from one interest to another

Leave an activity whenever feeling bored or become more interested in something else

Are curious & usually eager to try anything once

Smile & laugh a lot

Express emotions freely & are trusting

Are creative & innovative

Are physically active

Are constantly growing mentally & physically

Will risk often

They are not or are afraid to keep trying anything that they aren't initially good at & aren't afraid to fail

Rest when their body tells them to or if they resist, they become cranky

Learn enthusiastically & are passionate

Are open for coaching

Dream & imagine constantly

Still not sure if you need this book or if it will help you? Take the following need analysis.

If you answer "yes" to at least 5 of these questions, then it will help you & them.

If you answer "yes" to 8 or more there's NO DOUBT that you will benefit from this book.

1. You want your kids to grow up with the most confidence possible

   Y ____N____

2. You want your kids to be who they truly are

   Y ____N ____

3. You must tell your kids to do something more than THREE times before its done

   Y ____N ____

4. Your kids fight & argue often

   Y ____N ____

5. Your kids are afraid of the dark

   Y ____N ____

6. Your (new) significant other does not know much about your kids

    Y ____ N ____

7. Your kids are noisy when you need them to be quiet

    Y ____ N ____

8. You must make important phone calls when your kids are around

    Y ____ N ____

IF YES to at least five of above, skip to "Humble Beginning, if not then continue with the NEEDS ANAYSIS QUIZ

9. Your kids are overly competitive

    Y ____ N ____

10. You want to have a home safety plan

    Y ____ N ____

11. You need to get away from them without guilt

    Y ____ N ____

12. You "always" want to know who is in your kid's life

    Y ____ N ____

13. You want to get a pet for them but are not sure they are ready

    Y ____N ____

14. You would like them to "sometimes" play quietly

    Y ____N ___

15. You want some privacy with your spouse away from them

    Y ____N ____

    How did you do?

    If you answered NO to all fifteen, then thank you for your time & congratulations! Your kids may be perfect or robots! You will be the first member of the perfect Parent Museum.

    For those now with "YES" answers to at least five of the questions, go to & continue to Humble beginning & the other 101 ways you can accomplish your parenting goals for them & you

    They will provide fun, time-tested solutions & will work better than magic!

HUMBLE BEGINNING:

"I have to (or must) be smarter than these little kids" From a panicked uncle....ME!

60 Second Scream

The first time, I babysat my niece & nephews, I did not have a clue about what to do with them. My sister just told me to drive them to the local park & let them "play." Simple enough, yet every time we drove there, they were very noisy.

This was a kind of noise that was foreign to me. The only noise that was used while driving was the peaceful sound of jazz resonating through my stereo. Their noise was torture, the three of them in the backseat screaming & fighting. It sounded like a cross between cats & dogs fighting & World War III.

Once, I returned home & complained to my sister about the disaster, I learned that they were just doing what "little ones do."

Apparently, what "little ones do" were trying to drive me crazy & it worked. No matter what I tried in the car: bribes, pleading, threats, etc. nothing worked. They got louder & quickly figured it out. I was a rookie!

Then out of desperation & just before I completely lost it totally, I realized in spite of my upset, they were having a great (kid) time laughing (hopefully, not just at me). According to sis, they were being "normal." If this were "normal" I would be in big, big trouble.

Then a miracle happened… I "got it," I decided that I could have fun too! I was not going to be defeated by **FOUR- , FIVE- & SEVEN-year-olds**. I was going to attack rather than retreat.

So, the next time they were at the height of "playing," I blurted out:

"I WANT YOU TO SCREAM AT THE TOP OF YOUR LUNGS
& DON'T STOP FOR 60 SECONDS!

I had no idea where this approach came from, but something told me it had to be better than what was already happening. After astonished looks & whispers as to my sincerity… they did it. **They screamed!** I mean they gave it all that they had. If I thought there was noise before, I was mistaken.

That was a prayer meeting compared to THIS. **The difference was, now, I was in control!**

For the first time "they followed instructions." They started then stopped, started again, at my urging, until they had **screamed for sixty continuous seconds**. During the whole time of noisemaking (& after), they howled with laughter. What happened next was amazing. They fell completely silent for the rest of the trip.

I wondered, was this one-time good luck or just an aberration? Then the next time they were in my car they actually asked me if they could scream again for 60 seconds. Sure, I said.

They played my game with me again & the same results occurred. Now, I was certain I had stumbled onto something. It was my first time of really "being" with them.

It was not until many years later & many additional observations of other kids that I did it again. **Each time, I got the same results: Disbelief, Lots of Noise, Laughter & finally… QUIET.**

I am proud to put this as my first activity in … **"I Wasn't Kidding, Now, I Am."**

These **field tested** (by kids & parents) "activities"," games," "ploys" or whatever you wish to call them have been developed for parents & caretakers, including babysitters, uncles, grandparents & those who love just spending time with kids (henceforth called **TEAMMATES**), but don't want to surrender their sanity.

Now **TEAMMATES** can bond more often while **"the little ones"** develop their creativity & build their confidence. Although the basic foundation of the book is to have fun with them, it is also important to know that they help **establish boundaries & promote your personal family values.**

A true bonus is that the family values & lessons will continue far beyond the initial age range suggested. **The boundaries are taught using what I call "Love Based Discipline."**

This Discipline encourages them to do what you want & need them to do, while also showing your love for them.

How to BEST Use this Book

First

I highly recommend looking at the supplement entitled: **"GLOSSARY OF TERMS"**

This will help you in understanding & enhances your fun. I give credit where credit is due. This is really a collaboration of Ideas, methods developed by patience & love.

Next

Do not try to use this cover to cover. Use according to your priority & according to what you need or want to accomplish most.

"I Wasn't Kidding, Now, I Am"

Is not meant to be read from cover to cover but please read the table of contents, then pick out those activities as to your needs

There is no particular order of use but are recommended **to be used according to need & goal desired**

There are four distinct types of "Connecting Categories" **– Quick & Easy, Family Matters, Family Fun & Rewards**

Write, highlight, take notes, write all over this book

To make these tools and activities most effective TEAMMATES must go all out to get the best results. Halfway will get you less than half results. If you are naturally very reserved break loose or invite outgoing friend or family to participate

The age recommendations for kid participation are only recommendations for use. If you want to try different ages......by all means, go for it

Try THREE to FIVE a week (unless you can handle more) from distinct categories. Not everyone will fit or may be a success, but you will get impressive results from the majority. It is really up to you. Use your highest energy & best tone when giving directions. Best is to talk with a smile!!

I took liberty by having fun with some spelling, invented some innovative words (see GLOSSARY TERMS) at the end of the book. Lastly, forgive but I just had to replace all the words "and" with "&" because I just wanted to.

BENEFITS – You WILL receive some, most or all of the following

Parents & Kids

> **Will LEARN** to interact on a different & loving level with your kids
>
> **Will BE MORE** in tune with the brilliance & uniqueness of your child(ren).
>
> **Will DEVELOP A BOND** for a lifetime while maintaining your traditional family values
>
> **Will ENJOY REAL BREAKS** ranging from FIFTEEN minutes to an entire day
>
> **Will COMMUNICATE** more effectively with your children
>
> **WILL INSPIRE better behavior**: in grocery stores, restaurants or during friends' visits
>
> If this sounds really simple, it's because it is! Your kids will simply amaze you with their interest & willingness to play for learning.

Format Guide:

*PRACTICAL NONFICTION LITERATURE - Practical nonfiction is designed to communicate circumstances where the quality of writing is not considered as important as the content

PF = Parent Favorite,

TS = Time Saver,

PB = Parent Break

Connecting Categories

QE = Quick & Easy

Once you do it you can do it over & over without a lot of effort, it makes a little positive difference everyday

FTW = Family Teamwork

To reduce sibling rivalry, build trust & friendship (naturally)

FF = Family Fun

The whole family gets involved, mom & dad too

R = Reward

No free lunches, they get it when they get it, playing along benefits both you & them

Each

> Details who participate in addition to the child

Each

> Is setup in the same simple to follow format

Each

> Details an approximate time needed for completion

Participants

> **Kids aged 4 – 10**
>
> **Couples & Single Parents & Parents who work from home**
>
> **Significant Other (not the children's parent)**
>
> **TEAMMATES - Siblings, Playmates, Babysitters, Grandparents, Aunts & Uncles, Anyone who interacts with the children on an ongoing basis**

I wrote in a design & style for ease of understanding

You will notice incomplete sentences & purposeful lack of punctuation

I have also included directions as to what to say, ask or do for each interchangeable word as exercise, tool or activity

"NOTE"

> **Is stated before something that is particularly important to know**

> **Lastly, I've invented a number of new terms. So do not get hung up on the spelling.**

Ages: Recommended age to get the best results – not everything should be tried on every age

Use: When it is good is the time to use

Benefits: How should this effect problem

Materials: What is needed to provide for Connecting

Tidbits: Additional Helpful Tips

Results: What actual results to expect

BONUS: Extra goodies that come from this particular too

Concept Origination

> Where the idea for the activity came from

Good Luck, Have FUN, Make Memories & Create the Foundation YOU Want for YOUR Little Ones

Ok, that's enough of how & what they do! It is time to have fun & try them out!

Connecting Category #1
"Quick & EASY"

1. ### 60 Second Scream - **PF**
   Sometimes the best defense is a great offense

2. ### Hug Me
   If an apple a day helps, what about a hug?

3. ### Sit on Your Rear & Cheer
   They will never feel alone

4. ### MWA Kisses
   You will get as good as you give

5. ### Kissugs Count
   You madem, so you hugem

6. ### Hair, We Go
   When it is good to be a girl

7. ### Strike the Pose
   I see your feelings

8. ### All Shook Up
   Shake it, you can't break it

9. ### Tickle Me
   You tickle me every day in every way

10. ### Why Not
    This way today

11. Angel Secrets
They do have them too

12. Flip Flop
Another way of seeing the same thing

13. Monster Mash
You are my hero

14. I Squish Your Head
No need to get really mad

15. Cranky & Cruddy
Just one of those days

16. Made in the Shade **- PB**
Let the world go by

17. Praising
Never get tired of hearing it

18. Yes or No
The right answer

19. Why, WHy, WHY
You know let me know

20. See the Clock **- TS**
We keep our word

21. Speed Up
No need to be late, show the fun of being early

22. Signals **- PB**
I know when I can & cannot

23. Takeaway Awhile
But just awhile

24. No, NO, NOW **- TS**
I believe you

25. Mirror Me
You are the best reflection of me & you

#1 60 Second Scream – PF

Sometimes the best defense is a good offense

Ages   All

Use   Any time you want them to be quiet (for a later time ie.to a restaurant, a movie, etc.)

Benefits Helps relieve pent up energy

Tires them out

They are quieter than they would be (if suppressed)

Materials Ear plugs for you

Watch with a second hand

Tidbits   They must scream for 60 seconds as loud as they can

Instead of saying no to them, say yes

Results   Lots of laughter & amazing quiet

They will run out of gas & want to be quiet

Design   It may seem like a contradiction, having them scream to keep them quiet

(You will be pleasantly amazed, it works like a charm)

Tell them To scream as loud as they can for 60 seconds (best location is in your car - seriously). Join in (you'll see how tiring screaming is)

They will laugh when they realize that you really mean it & you let them go all out for it. You can always put ear plugs in your ears before you let them wail (do not worry you'll get the last laugh)

Make sure to time them for exactly for 60 seconds nonstop

If they stop before 60 seconds:

They must start over until they complete 60 seconds in a row (they should get it right by the third try)

It only works if they use up their energy

Encourage them to get louder & louder until they get all their energy out

60 seconds scream is much better then ongoing interruptions

Repeat total **60 SECOND SCREAM** *again if needed (quiet game great right after)*

#2 Hug Me

If an apple a day helps, what about a hug?

Ages   Best with multiple kids of all ages

Use   As often as you or they want

             At unexpected times

Benefits   Give & get love upon request

Materials Arms to hold them

Tidbits   Everybody hugs everybody

             Hugs even better when there is more than one child

Results   They will never grow out of wanting to give or receive a "**Hug Me**"

             The wanting will continue to the next generation

Design   "Requestor" **(R)** = Kid or parent

             "R" makes up a story in order to get a "**Hug Me**" (**HM** = a hug)

             "**HM**" is a story made of words that start with the initials of the "**R's**" first name

             Example: "**R**" = Kylie

                         "**R**" uses story words such as: Kites, Kaleidoscope, Kickers, Kangaroos,

             Keys, etc. that their words match their first name. Once a story is created then it remains the same using the same words to "request" a hug. *Hugs are given as soon as someone recognizes the story with words beginning with the letters of their first names*

It is fun when someone is caught off guard & doesn't catch on immediately

When you tell a story, then they know that you want a long **"Hug Me"** too

NOTE: **The first time you may have to go slow to make them realize that the story & the hug go together. YOU start using the first letter of your name (that is the key say Cathy – catching, carry, create, etc.)**

It does not take too long till they catch on

VARATION: Kids can start **"HM"** by asking questions that lead to the story (trying to catch you off guard)

Example #2

Hug wanted: Use first letter of child's name, say Emma Child starts a story about wanting to go to the zoo

Ask why? She responds: Because there are "Elephants" & "Eagles" & "Earthworms"

She will keep saying words that start with "E" until you ask for a **"HM"**

Sometimes, they are pretty clever when they ask

It might just go over your head for a minute

Do not worry; they'll let you know that they want an **"HM"**

Concept Origination

Do kids get enough hugs?

I love to hug; kids have always wanted to **"Hug Me,"** so it was not a stretch to produce a way to give & get a hug from them.

I wanted this sign of love to be given any place & any time. As a tease, I decided that a simple story had to be told by **"Requestor"** before they would get their hug. It became a way of getting **"two bangs for a buck** "a story & a hug."

BONUS: Smiles from parents & children

#3 Sit on Your Rear & Cheer

We are here to cheer you on!

Ages	6+
Use	Sporting events Recitals. Wherever they participate
Benefits	Shows love and support
Materials	The entire family & easily recognizable colored shirts
Tidbits	Cheer no matter what the results
	You will actually be the envy of many
	You will be seen rooting from anywhere in a crowd
Results	(After overcoming initial embarrassment) they will look forward to a roar above the crowd & have more fun & even stay in activities longer
Design	Whole family goes to an event that their kid is a **"Participant" (P)**
	Everyone else = **"Rooter" (R)**
	"P" picks
	A special color shirt that the family wears to show support & is easily seen by the **"P."**
	1st Time
	Tell "P(s)" - The shirt = love (no need to remind them again)

It may seem uncomfortable at first, standing, out, in the crowd but don't forget who it is for & why.

Root for the win, improvement, fun of participating

This reinforcement gives the **"P"** tremendous confidence, comfort, joy

They will know that no matter how they perform, they are special & loved

For multiple "P(s)" reverse roles of **"R"** & the **"P"**

NOTE: This is especially important because it truly builds a connection between them

Keeps them interested in each other & eliminates criticism of each other.

You are the leader, get out of your shell & yell "**P(s)**" always give their all!

Concept Origination

Shouldn't everyone be cheered on, at least for trying?

I watched a lot, I also participated, & I remember how it felt not having much family support at my sporting events.

I realized not everyone wins but everyone can & should feel good about participating.

The times my family did show up I felt pride & joy, knowing that they really cared! I also knew that by getting family support there was also a greater possibility that participating siblings would support each other far beyond their childhood years.

We have always been pretty loud so what would it look like if "supporters" took the lid off regardless of how well their little one(s) did.

BONUS: Shyness (what shyness?), Controlled Exuberance

#4 MWA Kisses – PF

(AKA Meaningful Welcome Always Kisses)

You will get as good as you give

Ages	All
Use	Any time anyone requests
Benefits	Have a lifetime of **MWA kisses**
Materials	Your energy
Tidbits	Be a good actor for each kiss
Results	Always, always special just for you & them
Design	First time you use this you have to sell it to them.
	Begin tomorrow morning right after breakfast
Tell them	That you will be giving them a **MWA Kiss**
	They are the only ones who get **MWA kisses** because they are special.
	Explain
	That **MWA kisses** can only be given between **TEAMMATES** & them (no one else)
Tell them	(In an excited voice) to run against the far wall to throw you a kiss
NOTE:	**You must get yours first to begin the magic:**
	They place their right hand over their mouths
	Turn their heads to the left.

Throw their right hand towards you

NOTE #2: **Key to success is FOR YOU to be an actress**

Act As though the kiss hits you in the face

(Actually, throw your head back & howl with pleasure)

Tell them That's how you "know" that the kiss is received (your head goes back)

After a few kisses from them, **throw a MWA kiss** to them

Tell them That they will feel it (if they throw their heads back too)

Throw one & Yell MWA!

They will automatically do their part

They will act like they have been hit by your kiss

Laughter will be a big part of this too

BONUS **You will be amazed how often that they will throw you a MWA kiss**

Concept Origination

I always love the connection between moms & their kids.

I wondered: how can I bring out that connection more often?

Then it came to me. I combined the good-bye kiss from a TV show called **"The Dating Game"** added the imagination of a child & the acting ability of loving parent.

The first time, I visualized everything in my mind first. Next, I described the **"MWA kisses"** process to my girlfriend. She tried it on her kids. It worked perfectly. It became a favorite for them & they never tire of it.

BONUS: Grandparents especially like them

#5 Kissugs Count

You madem, so you hugem"

Ages	All
Use	Very often
Benefits	Connects siblings & parents
	Helps them to be very affectionate
Materials	Arms to hold them & lips to kiss them
Tidbits	Don't leave home or go to bed without a kiss & a hug
	Make sure that they ask you before they hug any other non-related adult.
Results	Immediate love shared
Design	An activity you can start at the earliest age as a family norm
Feel	The benefits of being affectionate
	Be the lead
	It is very important to let them see simple signs of affection between you & your spouse (or partner).
	A simple kiss with partner
	Holding hands outside
	A hug for no reason
	Sitting together on the couch
	Hugging your friends when they come or go

NOTE: **This works best when you kiss & hug them for no reason**

Hugging in public is fine so do not hold back!

Tell them   They will never be too big to kiss & hug

Help them   Get used to knowing what they want & what they need from you (& eventually someone else)

It doesn't matter what your own family history was

If you have not done this in the past, do it now from now on

It gets easier & easier & feels better & better

It may take a while for it to become part of you if it is not already

Tell them   They are supposed to get at least three **"Kisshugs"** a day

If they do not get their 3 - They can ask for them!

NOTE: **Encourage them to keep track - the payoff is well worth it!**

#6 Hair We Go

When it's good to be a girl

Ages   All

Use   At least once a day

             Before special occasions

             Right before bedtime

             Especially when there is no time pressure or messy hair

Benefits   Shows the benefit of brushing hair

Materials Good brush & a soft touch

Tidbits   This precious time will be gone too quickly

             Take the time, just do it

             Do not make it stressful

             Let them brush your hair too

             Wash their hair while in the tub, sink or shower, make it extra special, a small new ritual

Results   Simple bonding that lasts a lifetime

Design

Make   Brushing hair, a ritual together.

             Although a simple task, take the time & space to slow things down even if only for a few minutes at a time.

             Gently, use your hand that is not brushing to stroke their hair.

Add a scalp massage for a minute or so (they
will love it).

Switch roles

NOTE: You will be in for an additional treat because of
the kind of conversations that develop during
this pampering break.

VARATION Learn how to French Braid then teach them

Make yourself available no matter what their
age

"Hair, We Go" is more of a "*being*" than a
"*doing*" activity

#7 Strike the Pose

Be *(positive) or not (positive) it really is up to them*

Ages   6+

Use   When they are being extraordinarily negative

Benefits   Expresses negative & positive feelings

Teaches them that they have a choice

They experience how negative & positive feelings look

Reinforces a positive experience

Reinforces a positive experience

Materials   Complete faith in the process

Tidbits   Actually do the poses.

It may not always be easy to be positive.

It will always feel better.

Results   They can always go to the happy pose whenever something negative is Happening. They always have the choice.

Design:

Help   Them to notice good & bad feelings in their bodies.

Have them   Face you @ arms-length away

FIRST pose = Negative emotion

Think of something that is painful or hurts.

Contort   Your body into a very tight tense bent over pose with matching facial expression.

Hold   Pose for a minute until you feel tired.

Tell them   How you feel (tense, tight tiring, etc.).

Repeat   While thinking of a bad thought.

Help them   Get tighter & tighter than hold for 30 seconds.

Ask them   How do you feel?

Then relax

Take   Deep breaths & shake it all out

SECOND pose = Positive emotion

Imagine   Something good happening or something that makes you happy

Convert   That to an incredibly open stance - arms raised.

Smile & spin Slowly in circles.

Laugh & hum

Take   FOUR or FIVE deep breaths

Tell them   The happy thoughts that you were thinking & how you feel

Now it is their turn!

Tell them   To talk about something that makes them happy, while their eyes are shut

Slowly move Their arms above their heads like a tree blowing in the wind

Tell them   To take 3 to 5 deep breaths as they move

Repeat   Happy thoughts & poses

Ask them   Again, how do they feel?

How it compares to negative thoughts poses & feelings

Repeat   Both poses & thoughts

#8 All Shook Up

Shake it - you will never - break it

Ages	All best with multiple kids
Use	If they are afraid or are upset
	Just before a performance or sporting event
Benefits	Gets in touch with the body
	Gets them out of bad mood
	Gets them into a state of relaxation
	Just for fun
Materials	Loose body & the alphabet
Tidbits	Go all out
	Do not hold back
	Shake your whole body
	Make a lot of noise
Results	They get into their body & out of their heads
Design	Be ready to step outside of yourself
Tell them	Do everything that you do to
Face them & take them	By their hands
Rotate	Headfirst to the left
	Next to the right

Finally in complete slow circles

Shrug   Shoulders up to your ears then drop them

Rotate   Arms in big circles while facing them

Shake   Each hand

Place   Your hand on your hips

Pull   In stomach way in & way out

Keep   Hands on hips

Rotate   Hips in large circles

Pick up   Left leg - shake about five times

Repeat

Pick up   Right leg

Shake   FIVE times

Shake   Each foot FIVE times

Once loose put it all together

Bend   Over loosely like a rag doll

Slowly stand straight up

Tell them   When you say "go:"

They have 30 seconds to shake everything at once (yell, encourage them)

Once they start, start yelling out the various parts to shake: the left leg, the hips, shake, shake, shake, it until you say stop

Repeat   For TWO more "Shake It" rounds

Their mood will absolutely change (so will yours)

Tell them   When scared they can shake all the bad stuff out in less than a minute!

#9 Tickle Me

You tickle me very day in every way

Ages   All

Use   Bedtime, nap time, or morning

Benefits   Relaxes them with gentle wind down

Materials   Time & tenderness or until they fall asleep

Tidbits   Touch them gently with love, on their face, arms & legs.

Results   They bond & trust you

Design   Tenderness to build a bond that will last

Tell them   To shut their eyes & think happy thoughts while you tell them going a fairy tale

Lightly touch Their face, neck, arms & legs while telling fairy tale

Combine light touches, soft talk with telling them how much you love them & how you will always make them safe.

Concept Origination

Are there really more (good) ways to skin a cat?

I have always been curious. Even doing things the same way can seem different with a different mindset. The idea was to see things through new eyes to allow creative ideas to grow.

There would also be so much more to share. So, the activity blossomed. No trip was ever the same, even if the same route was chosen every day.

BONUS: New ideas will flourish

#10 Why Not

This way…. for today

Ages   6+

Use   Small choices can make a unique experience

Benefits Gets you out of your normal mindset

Breaks patterns

See what the other choice would look like

Helps them look at things from different perspectives too

Materials Quick thinking

Tidbits   Don't think too much

Go with the new fun

When you recognize an old pattern try another way

Results   Magic created by getting out of routine or comfort zone

Design

Develop   A practice of mixing things up for fun

Really help them to make a different choice instead of just doing the same activity the same way.

Alternative choices will attract:

New feelings

Emotions

Understanding

Awareness to the same (boring or unnoticed) routine

Routine Alternative

Taking same way to school or take a longer way

Listening to same radio show then spice it up & sing

Turning TV to the same show or watch a foreign film

Coming right home after school then go to an early movie as a treat

Say no to anything then last minute say yes

Enroll your children into **"Why Not"**

It will help to minimize the phrase "I just don't want to" when asked if they would like to try something new.

#11 Angel Secrets

For you & for them

Ages	5+ (especially good when starting school. It helps you to keep informed)
Use	You want them to feel extra special
Benefits	Keeps secrets just between you & them
Materials	Mom & dad, them, post it notes, special Angel secrets' box
Tidbits	Builds trust & also share for a lifetime
Results	They will share both fun & important things with you that they may not have otherwise shared for fear that others will find out.
Design	You (later they) grab air into your hand call out **"Angel Secrets" (AS)**
Tell them	**"Angel Secret"** is only for them because they are Angels & you love them.
	Once you call **"Angel Secret,"** they will know you are going to tell them something special.
	This is a fantastic way to get their attention or calm them down.
	They will listen because they are getting your full attention.
	It is easy to create **"Angel Secrets."** Simply use at least 1 of 5 questions in the AS - Who, What, Where, When & Why

Write the simple ones on post it notes then place in special Angel Box

Examples: After whom they were named?

What is your favorite color?

What was your favorite pet as a child?

Where did you go on vacation?

Why do they have their middle names? Who is your best friend?

Ask them   If they have any "Angel Secrets" for me

Concept Origination

Are our first reactions always the best?

I was encouraged many years ago to see things from a different perspective. As a simple reminder to look at situations differently each day, I remembered to take the first step of the day with the other foot. Crazy but it worked & it put me in a different mindset, the day was different.

My idea was to do the same with the brain; We know how we normally act.

BONUS: New creativity may (& will) appear

NOTE: **That's how I came to author this book. I got OUT OF THE BOX & realized it didn't have to be perfect to be effective**

#12 Flip Flop

It is not what happens, it's what happens NEXT that counts

Ages   All

Use   Life comes at you or them in a negative way

When a small crisis happens:

Things get spilled

Knees get scrapped

Feelings get hurt, etc

If you feel frustrated & upset

They seem scared or are being very defensive

You notice a certain look in their eyes

`It is time to **"Flip Flop"** your reaction

Benefits   Keeps you sane & better focus on what is really important

Materials   An open mind

Tidbits   React in the opposite way than what is typical

Results   More laughter

Calmer reactions to the situation

Much less stress for you & them

Design   No one needs to tell you that **"Stuff"** happens (with more than one child **"Stuff"** happens all the time).

Allow the imperfections of the day without undue stress caused from the **"Stuff."**

The point of **"Flip Flop"** is not to worry about "what happens" but to focus on your (& their) "reaction to it."

"Flip Flop:" "Stuff" happens

Before reacting:

Stop, then try the opposite reaction (instead of "knee jerk" reaction)

Normally: When **"Stuff"** happens, it is viewed as a crisis:

"Knee Jerk Reactions" - Yelling, Blaming, Anger, Frustration & Impatience

Feelings of Victimization - Why this? Why now?

Now: When **"Stuff"** happens, it is viewed as part of "normal" life:

"Flip Flop Reaction"

Pause

Take three deep breaths

Check for injuries

Thank God no one is hurt (or hurt too badly)

Little to nothing said, move on

No Blame

"Hug Me" given

Tell them "What You Want"

The lesson learned from the experience

Give them "**Points**" if they can repeat what you just **said**

NOTE: This all goes out the window if it is serious or child is totally upset at that time & then just hug them!

Sometimes a combination of each (**"stuff"** happens) you are only human ☺

Make sure to end on an "UP" note!

BONUS: Your mindset will shift to a more positive one & you will have easier & more control

There's always more than one way to react to "**STUFF**"

#13 Monster Mash

**The day they were born you
became their "Monster Masher"**

Ages	All as needed
Use	You see a mood change before bedtime
	They try to sleep with you too often
	They cry for no good reason at night
	You notice that they have a fear of going to bed
	Immediately if they wake up afraid during the night
Benefits	Alleviates fears of monsters in their room or an overactive imagination
Materials	**"Monster Mash"** tools – broom, large pair of shoes & a flashlight
Tidbits	Be the hero/spend the time needed to reassure them
	Ham it up in a way while you **"Mash the Monster"**
Results	Less "lifetime" fears, fears such as, Fear of the dark or fear of the unknown
Design	For many reasons monsters become part of a kids growing up.
	Sometimes monsters appear after interacting with others - meaningful relatives, friends or even babysitters.

Tell them that you were also afraid of the **BOOGIEMAN** under your bed.

Then your mom & dad got rid of him. Now you do not have anymore fear of the **BOOGIEMAN**

Nip   Fears in the beginning build trust & pay big dividends for you & them.

Time spent being the **"Monster Masher"** will be well spent.

Explain   What a **"Monster Masher" (MM)** does & when they can call for one to get rid of the **BOOGIEMAN**

As soon as they ask you to **"Mash the Monster"**

Be outrageous

Declare that "You are the Best **"Monster Masher"**

Show   Your unique **"MM"** technique

Make something up

Add to it (as you go)

Be noisy

Tell them   That your **"MM"** gets rid of all the monsters

Make them   Friendly, not scary (whichever way they believe is ok)

Ask them   Where can you help? Under the desk, under the bed or in the closet

Where do they think the Monster is?

What does he look like?

Use "MM"	Grab broom – sweep it under the bed as you make loud noises
	Talk to them & the monster
Ask	What is going on?
Tell them	What "you" see (be "way out" there). Monster running out of the door or out the window far away
Act	Like a wild superhero (it is important & will get them laughing!)
Play	As long as they need you too
Ask	Is it gone?
	Is it now friendly?
	Only when they say "yes" do you stop.
INSIST	To do it also with the lights on
	End with a big hug & tuck in.
NOTE:	**It is ok to keep the "monster" protector night light on**
Create	**"Monster Mash"** song that will also do the work
	They can always play the special song when they need to
	Assure them that you will never let any monster hurt you or anyone else

Concept Origination

How do some kids overcome the monsters & others do not?

I always liked the thought of being a hero for kids. What better way to be the hero than to make the **"boogie man"** go away? Where did boogie men come from? I sure wished someone would have mashed them for me. So now you get to mash them for them. Be their hero.

NOTE: **Here is where parent heroes are made**

#14 I Squish Your Head

Less frustration more fun for them

Ages	All
Use	Something is bothering them
	For fun
	To change moods
	To release frustration
Benefits	Relieves frustration without being destructive
	Lots of laughs
Tidbits	Use instead of hitting someone
	Use instead of keeping bad feelings inside
	Kids can play alone
Results	They learn to relieve bad feelings without hurting anyone or keeping it inside
	They also learn – **"I Squish Your Head"** causes no harm
Design	They use, their **"Right "Squish Your Head Hand"**
	(The *left hand won't work - it's the rule*!)
	"Squish Your Head" technique - make backward letter **"C"** with the right hand
Curl	Last three fingers into the palm, point thumb & first finger like your saying: it is only "this big"
Next:	They close their right eye (yes, more rules)

Now: Point two fingers at a faraway object

Frame object or person's head

Say magic words (as you open & close the fingers repeat). THREE times:

I "Squish Your Head"

I "Squish Your Head"

I "Squish Your Head"

NOTE: **Great for kids in a car to keep them busy**

Valuable if something or someone is bothering them

When they say they are **"Squishing** (someone's) **Head,** it gives you a heads up that that person is bothering them

This will also alert you that something might need to be taken care of at an early stage before they withdraw, become afraid, or take physical action against someone (even a sibling)

Concept Origination

Could there be a good kid stress reliever?

I saw this on a television show many years ago.

An old guy sitting on a bench in a park would **"Squish Heads"** when people bothered him. He would use his first finger & thumb to frame those bothering him & then "squish them" by squeezing the fingers together, strange but funny.

I noticed how many children suppressed anger & who ended up taking it out on a little brother or sister.

Somehow the **"Squish Your Head"** idea re-emerged. Since it was harmless, the **"Squish Your Head"** technique could be used to let off steam when something upsets them.

I could also see very quickly what it was that was causing the upset.

I remember seeing my nephew upset about something, so I explained to him about

"Squishing Heads." First, I explained the purpose of squishing heads then I explained that nobody really got hurt, he loved it. Later, when something bothered him, he would **"Squish heads,"** right then & there.

There is no longer any unnecessary build up or misdirected anger. Once he could vent his frustrations, he picked on his little sister & brother much less.

NOTE: **Less (physical) is more rewarding**

#15 Cranky & Cruddy

To be or not to be - either way - is ok

Ages	6+
Use	At least 1 of them is being **"Cranky & Cruddy"**
	When you are at wits end
Benefits	Changes bad mood
	Teaches them about choice
	Lessons duration of bad mood
Materials	At least ONE **Cranky Cruddy Kid & Cranky Cruddy** List
Tidbits	Do not pick on them but acknowledge
	Don't baby them
	Let them be by themselves
Results	They choose their mood (for limited amount of time)
	They move on
Design	
Announce	To group that someone is being **"Cranky & Cruddy" (CC)**
	Everyone must leave you alone with the **"CC kid"**
Tell	CC
	That they must answer 10 Cranky questions in order to be officially **"Cranky & Cruddy"**

Are you sleepy?

Do you feel well?

Is something bothering you?

Did someone hurt you?

Do you want to go to bed?

Would you like to cry?

Would you like to laugh?

Would you like a hug?

Would you snuggle together for a few minutes?

Are you hungry or dirty?

Tally up   Answers

They must say yes to at least six answers to be **"Officially CC"** otherwise they are just one (C) or the other (C)

If not, then they have to give you a reason to make them **CC**

Watch   For laughter

Once they are laughing

Tell them   They are not **CC** so they can start playing with the others again

If there is no laughter or they have answered yes to at least SIX questions

Tell everyone

> That they are **"Officially Cranky & Cruddy"** **(OCC)**
>
> Once officially **OCC**
>
> They have three choices:
>
> Any choice is ok but only one will be chosen.
>
> #1. Get up to 1 hour to act as **OCC** as they want no one will stop them or give them grief, but after **FIFTEEN** minutes they must stop (use "**See the Clock**")
>
> #2 Accept that they are just one of the ten & don't need to spend **FIFTEEN** minutes being **OCC**
>
> #3 Invite everyone to be OCC with them, they are the **OCC Boss**

NOTE: **If there is a deeper upset, stop the game, go into the bedroom & just hold them tight**

Tell them   It is always ok to be **OCC,** but they do have a choice not to be

> That you love them even when they are **OCC**
>
> When they are done being **OCC** then the good things will begin

#16 Made in the Shade – PB

Really having it made in the shade

Ages	All
Use	Any afternoon & when the summer heat is too much
Benefits	Keeps energy level low, slows everyone down & creates a quiet time
Materials	Big shady tree
	A bed sheet
	Picnic (light food)
	Personal journal
	Books
	Pants (to fray)
	Board games
Tidbits	Keep it simple & slow
Results	Fun no matter how hot
Design	
Find	The biggest shade tree you can within a few miles of your home
Make	It a game of being under the shade of the tree
Tell them	They can go anywhere the shade is, but they cannot leave its boundaries
	To play board games
	To tell stories

To look into the sky & describe any clouds

To Bird watch, etc.

Have them   Write down all that they see under the shade

Move with the shade & hang in there until it is twilight

#17 Praising

Get more with honey than with vinegar

Ages	All
Use	Very often
Benefits	Give & receive praise
	Learn the feeling giving without expectations of receiving
	Acknowledging the good in someone by telling that person
Materials	Poster board & pen for their list
Tidbits	Accept humbly
	Acknowledge confidently
	Give from the heart
Results	They learn to look at the good
Design	
Tell them	That you will also praise them for doing the right thing

"Praising"

P	**= Personal - from you to them**
R	**= Repeatedly – over & over**
A	**= Authentic - from the heart**
I	**= Intentionally - do not be shy**
S	**= Simple - the good in others is easy to see**

I	**= Initiate - it happens when you make it happen**
N	**= Naturally - if you see it acknowledge it**
G	**= Graciously - do it because it' the right thing to do**

Make   A list of actions to praise

Who have they praised?

Their friends, people that you let them talk to

When others praise them

Praise them for simple things such:

Brushing their hair

Being nice to each other

Asking politely

Completing homework, etc.

Goals: Find FIVE different things to praise them for every day

Find FIVE things they praise someone else for every day

Give   Points for writing down when they were praised, or they praised someone else.

Go   Over their list once a week (during **Family Matters**)

NOTE: **Give weekly or monthly rewards for their efforts**

#18 Yes or No

The answer is always there

Ages	6+
Use	Anytime, anywhere
Benefits	Reduce or eliminate the "I don't know" answers
Materials	Three fingers
Tidbits	Trust the answer
	No thinking required
	Make decisions when the choices are about the same
Results	Quick reliable answers
Design	When they say "I don't care" to your questions, they must pick "Yes or No"
	If they still cannot choose, then you will give them a way to get the answer
Explain	That inside themselves they always know the right answer
Touch	The tip of the first finger the tip of the thumb of the left hand – hold fingers as tightly as possible (like you are making the OK sign)
	For "**Yes**" response from this for the magic circle
Give them	A question that you 100% know that the answer is yes

Example: Is your name...? (They say their name.)

Now put the entire first finger of the right hand into the circle.

Tell them To pull hard to break the connection between the thumb & the finger (they will stay together)

For "NO" ask

A question you know that the answer is 100% NO

Repeat: Pull the fingers apart

Again ask A question they originally said "I don't know" to the answer the answer will now easily appear, really!

NOTE: **Next time, they don't care whether the answer is A or B use this simple but effective tool, it works!**

Use it for yourself when you are trying to decide – "Chicken or Fish"

#19 Why, WHy, WHY

Not just why, why not

Ages   5 - 8

Use   You are asked **"why"** about something & there needs to be more depth

Benefits They come to you for answers

Materials Your patience

Tidbits   Be more curious

Address the question as an opportunity to learn & teach

Go deeper than the first question

Don't get stopped

Be curious

Have more awareness, internet connection, computer & telephone

You do not always have to tell them a serious answer; it can be just for fun

You may not always know the answer, but you will help them find out

Results   Trust is built

Design: As your kids grow, they will become more & more curious.

They will want to know an answer about everything, the **"Whys"** will begin.

The **"Whys"** might come at the most inopportune times or at the best time.

You will become aware of the opportunity to connect.

Encourage Them to come to you when they need to know something

Use Your own knowledge

Books at hand

The library

The internet

Call up Someone you know who may know the answer

Once you give them a truthful answer, it is their job to remember it (as best they can)

NOTE: **This works best by having them share the answer with someone as soon as possible (siblings or other parents work great for this).**

RULE: They can only ask you "Why" 3 times in a row for the same question

While she got what she wanted more time to complete what she needed to do plus have more time with me? A thought came to mind.

For years, I heard other parents say to their kids "I'll be with you in 5, 10 or 15 minutes." No matter what, they would always come back in just a few minutes. They did not understand the concept of time. The number of minutes mentioned by the parents meant nothing to them.

This was a problem that wasn't unique. I looked at the situation from their point of view: They wanted attention - they were not trying to interrupt just for interruption's sake & they did not like being lied to when they were kept being put off.

From that **"See the Clock"** was born.

The beauty of this idea was that they didn't have to be able to tell time for it all to work.

All they had to do was to see the hands of a clock.

#20 See the Clock - PB/TS

A break for you - fun for them

Ages　　　5+

Use　　　When you need 15 minutes for a phone call

　　　　　For high priority task that requires only 15 minutes

Benefits　　Trust is built (they trust you)

　　　　　Phone calls completed quicker

　　　　　FIFTEEN-minute tasks don't become longer tasks

　　　　　No more yelling because everyone's needs are taken care of

Materials　Visible clock that has numbers & it has second hand

Tidbits　　They do not have to read or understand time

　　　　　It does not work for longer tasks

　　　　　You must let callers know your need to stick to 15 minutes

　　　　　Stick to your part; You must get off the phone after 15 minutes

Results　　They interrupt less often

　　　　　The phone is no longer a competitor for their attention

Design:　　Do you remember the last time you became frustrated when your children kept interrupting you during an important phone call?

Did you yell at them not to interrupt?

Did you tell them that you would be with them in five minutes, but the five minutes stretched into much longer because they just kept coming right back?

Do simple tasks sometimes never get completed or take too much time?

If you answered yes to any of these questions, then this will help in a big way

Your Old Point of View (POV)

A simple call may take hours to complete due to constant "kid" interruptions

All you need is FIFTEEN uninterrupted minutes to complete your call

You become frustrated, drained & not happy with them

Their Old POV

Time doesn't mean anything

NOTE: **They are only kids - give them a break**

Call them   To you

Tell them   That you have to make a phone call for FIFTEEN minutes

You will be playing a game called **"See the Clock"**

The game is they cannot interrupt you during the call

When your call is finished then you will give them 100% of your attention

When you get on the phone, they look at the numbers on the clock

Point out Where the hands will be in 15 minutes

Their part To go play & not to come back until the hands are touching the number you showed them.

Your part

Complete Your call in 15 minutes - no more!

Get off The phone when they come back

Give them 100% of your attention

Tell them They can only come back early if there is an emergency (define emergency)

When the hands-on the clock are in the right place, come back & stand in front of you

Keep an eye on that clock because your kids will be testing your integrity!

NOTE: **THIS WILL NOT WORK if you delay getting off the phone after FIFTEEN minutes.**

It is extremely important for you to keep your end of the bargain

It will work like a charm if you give them your full attention when the time is up

It is fun for them & is a great way to keep sane in FIFTEEN-minute increments.

Time limits can be extended as they get older.

They will love it & so will you!

You can ask for multiple FIFTEEN minutes after you give them 100% for their needs right then (sometimes they forget what they wanted (oh darn)

Concept Origination

Can you use time breaks without kids actually knowing how to tell time?

This was created out of necessity, just like the **"60 Second Scream."** The idea came during my long-distance relationship with my girlfriend.

Selfishly, I wanted a few undisturbed minutes with her on the phone without abusing or neglecting her kids.

I learned during my conversations with her that throughout the day, many tasks that would normally take fifteen uninterrupted minutes seemed to take hours. There was a great deal of frustration for all involved if they constantly interrupted.

How could I get what I wanted?

I wanted a bit more time with her on the phone.

Did they get what they wanted attention?

When they came up as always, they were told that they were to leave mom alone until the little hand (on the big clock) hit a certain number, they understood that. Magic happened immediately.

They left mom alone without arguments or wasted time. As long as mom stuck to her part of the bargain by getting off the phone, there was no further need for her to yell. She got her 15 minutes of freedom, finished many more tasks without interruption & I was able to talk to her without guilt.

NOTE: The simplicity of this is that it is really about integrity & trust. When mom pointed to the clock & said that she would be with them when the hand hits fifteen, mom HAS to stick to her part of the bargain. The "trust" is why it works so well.

Also NOTE: It is not very effective for times over 30 minutes.

#21 Speed Up

No need to be late, they learn the fun of being early!

Ages	6+
Use	When they need to get up at odd times
	You know that it will be tough getting them up to get them someplace quickly
Benefits	Get them from point A to point B quickly (before they realize what hit them)
Materials	Whistle or noise makers & sense of humor
Tidbits	Use high energy & a happy loud voice
	Let them sleep on the long drive or plane ride
	Have kids shower the night before
Results	Up & out much faster
Design:	To get them up fast with no whining
Tell them	The night before that you will play **"Speed Up."**

Next morning

Call out	loudly **"Speed Up"** you have 5 minutes then begin to count down
Turn on	Lights
Strip off	bed covers
Cheer them	On to get their pre laid out clothes
	One parent helps them dress quickly.

NOTE: **Speed & your happy energy is important**

Gets them going before they know what has hit them

Look At your watch & call out times

Be A cheerleader

Once they get going, they will laugh. **PROMISE**

#22 Signals – PB

Signal the right time for everything

Ages	5+
Use	To get privacy with your partner every day
Benefits	No guilt for you or resentment to them
Materials	Home-made (construction paper) traffic sign
	Green, red & **yellow** circles
	Pair of scissors & glue
Tidbits	
Show	Color to equal meaning that you want them to see
Give them	Sheet with meaning beside each color
Take them	In the car to show them how a traffic light works & how everyone obeys the color rule
Then compare	
	It to your home signal
	Once they understand the meaning of the colors, bring it home
Results	They know when to come in or not
	You get space & time
Design:	To get some privacy in your own bedroom
Make	Paper stop light
Place	It on your bedroom door

Give them   A situation list = color for each (**red**, **yellow** or **green**)

Red = Come in only if you are dying

Yellow = Knock & wait/we will come out or let you in

Green = Count to 10 aloud then come in

Tell them   They must obey your sign

How much fun they will have by looking at the signals

When you need a break or alone time simply uncover the color you want

You can always be flexible as you want - It really works

Concept Origination

Can parents still have privacy? I saw something similar to this used with a friend of mine in his business. His staff knew exactly if & when they could interrupt him. By using this stop sign idea, he was able to have a very successful business with only planned interruptions.

Another fact I realized was how many parents say that they never have a few minutes with each other. I really believe in keeping the connection between parents.

I do not believe it's all for they & nothing for the grownups. It is the Libra in me, I want balance.

NOTE: **A time to stop, a time to go & a time to go with caution too**

#23 Takeaway Awhile

You can "giveth," sometimes you must "taketh" away

Ages   5+

Use   Discipline - as a last resort

Benefits   They will get the message

Materials   Your strong will & consistency

Tidbits   Pick item important enough to them that if taken away will cause them to do the right thing so not to lose the item

Give them   A last chance before taking the item(s) away.

Hold   Item (s) at least 24 hours

Results   Better behavior or at least shorter bad behavior times

Design: There are consequences for bad actions

                When they are acting up

                They (or you will) must pick out a favorite item that is going to be put "in storage" until they can buy it out with good behavior

                Know their favorite Toy, Book, Skirt, Shirt, T-shirt, Jewelry Piece, Movie, Pillow, Doll

Be   Firm, they can pick THREE items, but you have the ultimate choice.

                They will not like that their "favorite" is gone

                They will want to earn it back as soon as possible

Concept Origination

Would all kids pay attention & mind you when you needed to more often if you took away what really was important to "them"?

Boundaries, kids need them (deep down they want them). Using the same techniques for disciplining each kid just did not seem to work. I found that by knowing what was important to the individual child made all the difference in the world for discipline. It also keeps their attention.

Without consequences, I saw good kids become monsters. I saw good babysitters lose control. By taking what is important from a kid for just awhile, boundaries are set & respected without a great deal of Upset. Now the parents save a lot of time & energy.

NOTE: **Without can be fun too**

#24 no, NO, NOW – TS

What part of "No" do you not understand?

Ages	All
Use	They keep pushing you
Benefits	They get the message & take action without testing you
Materials	Your strong will to end "discussion"
Tidbits	Stick to your guns
Results	You save time
	No more war of wills
Design:	Sometimes they test your willpower in many direct & not so direct ways.
	By using **no, No, NOW** you always win.
Tell them	When you say **"no, No, NOW"** there will be no more discussion.
	They will do what you say, that's it!
	Any more grief from them will cause them to lose "Points" get **"Kid**
	Correction" or go directly to their room until you decide they can come out.
	Once you say **no, No, NOW**
	You will save a lot of time & energy
	Have fun!
Example	To turn off the TV & go to bed

They say Ok in five minutes in order to finish (which is not unreasonable) Remember **Watch the Clock"**

You respond Ok but that you do not want any arguments

FIVE minutes later - you come back

Tell them It is time

IF they begin to fuss & plead for more time

Normally, additional frustration begins that goes on & on

Now, say "no, NO, NOW" = end of discussion

Hold up Your hand, without any further comment

Shut off The TV

Take them To bed

It does not matter about their rants & tantrums

Put them In their room

Shut Their door

NOTE: **It does not matter whether they take their clothes off or not**

The key is don't keep the conversation going but take necessary action

Concept Origination

Can kids really listen? It seemed like half the time mom was saying "no" many times with little effect. This helps moms stick to the important nos.

NOTE: **They will know when you are serious**

#25 Mirror Me

You are the best reflection of me & you

Ages   5 - 8

Use   Every THREE or FOUR months

Benefits   Helps to develop self-esteem

Materials Full length mirror

Tidbits   Do with workout clothes

Or more naturally in the nude

One on one with each child

Results   They feel special for who they are

Design: To provide a natural way for mom with the girls' dad with the boys to help them be comfortable with whom they are

Use   This way before there can ever be an issue of your children being uncomfortable with their bodies.

Just stand there

Play   (A slow bit of) monkey see monkey do

Start   From the top of the head to the bottom of your feet

NOTE: **Take the time to stand in front of the mirror**

Really look at yourself with them & them at themselves with you

If for any reason being in the nude is not right for you then wear body type workout clothing, or bathing suit so the body is in its closest natural look.

This is not a time to try to look good.

It is a time to explain to them the similarities & differences between your body & theirs

Pick them   Up

Talk   To them

Encourage   Them to feel good about themselves, now just mention that no one is perfect

Questions

You will be setting the stage for them to feel good about themselves

By practicing "Mirror Me" you will go a long way to eliminate any future upsets that could have been caused by peers, boy/girlfriends, etc.

They will become as comfortable as you are

ALSO: Explain the difference between this & having someone else see them

Each time they do this, they know how you feel about them

They will love to be measured to know that they are getting to be "Big"

Connecting Category #2
"Family Teamwork"

26. Pass Off - PB & PF
When 1 +1 = 3

27. Remember When
Nothing good is ever forgotten

28. Mad About You – PF
A natural feeling

29. Grooving w/Grandparents - PB & PF
I am so glad when you come

30. Caring Catch Up - PF
We want you to know about us

31. Separate X Love
We both still love you

32. Kitchen Wonders – PF
Teach me, I want to know

33. Mom/Dad's Work
Just for you

34. Mine, Yours, Ours
One for all & all for one

35. Tag Team - PB & PF
We do it for you

36. Come on Over
I like my friends

37. Heaven Yes
Here in my mind

38. Space Time - PB & PF
Taken for love's sake

39. Time 2 Talk
Time to learn what we need to know

40. Talkus
We learn from each other

41. Impressions
What they mean to me

42. Boundaries
Taking it to the limit

43. Hard As
I do not have to be

44. Doctor Buddy
He helps me when I am sick

45. Kid Power
The power from you

46. Clean Up - TS
Here's how it's done

47. Master Rules - PF
You are the boss

#26 Pass Off - PB & PF

We appreciate all that you do & we are a team

Ages	All
Use	To show appreciation & to give a break
Definitions	(Frazzled) "**Homemaker Inside Parent**" = HIP
	"**Outside Working Parent**" = OWP
Benefits	"**HIP**" gets a break by reversing role with "**Outside Working Parent**" (OWP) for a day.
	Kids & "**OWP**" show respect to "**HIP**"
	They learn not to be so messy (they know that they will have to clean up)
Materials	Cleaning stuff
	Rubber gloves, etc.
	Fun music
	Alarm clock
	"**Pick it up**" energy
Tidbits	"**A loving gift**" not a task & everyone uses rubber gloves
	Place some fun surprises for them as they clean (i.e.. candy)
Results	Makes mundane becomes fun
Design:	"**HIP**" Goes out & does whatever she "(or he) wants (min. 4 hrs.)
	"**OWP**" Puts fun music on & gets kids to help clean each room

Organizes everyone to work together

Makes cleaning to be a fun adventure

Gets them to help make dinner

It is not about how good everything is done (in the beginning)

More about doing something together

Gives them the feeling they are helping

Hopefully, some actual chores are being done such as: dishes, making beds, dusting, cleaning bathrooms & laundry (are good places to start)

Concept Origination

How to appreciate the **"inside" (home) spouse** for what they do in the home?

How to express that to that spouse & them?

I also imagined how damaging it was to kids to hear resentment from one spouse because of lack of appreciation. Since kids take in so much more than sometimes realized, why not show the value of the **"inside" (home) spouse (from everyone**) & give the **"inside**" (also working) parent" a break?

No matter whether it is the man or the woman, the value is still the same. I say show respect for both roles & teach that respect to the children.

NOTE: **Important work does not always come with money.**

#27 Remember When

Let the good times roll & roll again

Ages   7+

Use   Times of upset

If there is talk about something being "hard"

You hear them use the phrase "I never or I can't replace with I can not not yet"

Benefits   It gives them courage or faith to overcome a present situation such as: divorce, unwanted move, sickness

Gets them out of their upsets

Materials Your memory

Tidbits   Be clear about past good times (if the present is not good)

Dig deep, do not rush anything

Remember "good things" that happened last week, last month or a long time ago

Results   They learn that the present is not always good, but it will be again

They learn that the present is not always good, but it will be again

Design: Many times, when there is something upsetting to children, the good times become a distant memory or seem like they never even occurred.

When there are upsets:

> They are sick for a few days
>
> Family Separation
>
> Divorce
>
> Death of loved one pet or friend
>
> When these upsets dominate the mood, ask them to
>
> **"Remember When"** _____
>
> **"Remember When"** _____
>
> (Fill in with *fun time that they have had, places they've gone, etc. & talk of the future good times that will be coming).

Help them   To **"Remember When"** to take their "now" reality

Limit   Their "exaggeration" of bad periods by put things in perspective

#28 Mad About You – PF

OK - *get angry…. then let it go!*

Ages   6+

Use   They get mad & decide they have to be

Benefits   Allows child to be mad at you then get over it in a shorter time

Materials Patience & time & space

Tidbits   Don't let them take the anger to bed

Results   They learn choices: to be mad & let it go or be mad & stay mad

Design: They get mad, it is ok

They also need to understand that "staying there" is not the place to be - let them be mad… for a while.

Once a reasonable amount of **"Mad time"** has passed discuss need & benefit of letting it go & not staying mad.

When first mad

Ask   What exactly are they mad at right now?

Acknowledge

Then explain That they cannot always get their own way

Share   Times when you did not get your way & how it benefited to you

After the worst has passed:

Talk   Softly with them

Don't push it, the first few times will take longer to get over.

Ask   Do you want to stay mad?

Why did they not get their way?

Say   It is ok but they will feel better if they don't

That you love them very much even when they are mad

Explain: It is ok "**Being Mad**"

It's Unhealthy **"Staying Mad"**

It is healthy to **"Letting Go"**

Examples: **Being Mad** - ball up your right hand into a fist as tight as you can (they do the same thing).

Hold   It tight for FIFTEEN seconds

Ask   How does their hand feel?

Staying Mad

Continue   Holding for at least FORTY-FIVE seconds –

Ask   How does it feel now?

Letting Go   Open your hand & wiggle your fingers

Ask   Which feels better?

Being Mad   While using **"Strike the Pose"** in front of a mirror

NOTE: **Pictures of people being angry examples work well. They get them out of their mood faster once they see some of the outrageous ways people look when they are upset**

Pictures of People **"Staying Mad,"** what it looks like to others

Themselves both "Being Mad" & **"Letting Go"**

People **"Letting Go"** (happy people) = especially

Them or someone they know

Place them In front of a mirror

Have them Make a "mad face" & Hold it 15 seconds

Then release

Say "This is how they look to others when they are mad"

How does that feel?

How does it look?

Staying Mad

Keep holding the frown

"How does it feel?"

"How does it look now?"

Letting Go

Release The frown

Make Silly faces

Smile (They will laugh)

Ask Which feels better?

NOTE: **It is important to let them come to a conclusion without coaching**

Reassure them

That everyone gets mad sometimes

It is ok to be mad for a while but when they want to feel better, they have to let go - They always have a choice

Concept Origination

Can kids be ok with getting mad but just for a while?

Since all emotions are natural. Sometimes, kids do get angry, so do moms & dads.

Being in hot water for a while seemed better than going to the boiling point. After a little goes by it makes "making up" nicer for them.

They now know that having their good & bad feelings are ok.

NOTE: **Letting off steam is always good & healthy**

"When children are allowed to express their anger, they bring a very healthy attitude about it through their adult years and therefore usually move through their anger very quickly."

(Conversations with God, Book 3, Neale Donald Walsch)

#29 Grooving w/Grandparents GPs - PB & PF

Play has no age

Ages	All
Use	Whenever grandpa & grandma are up for it (**GPs**)
Benefits	Brings back the youth of your parents
Tidbits	Keep activities within the realm for the older playmates
	Enroll **GPs** into being childlike with their grandchildren
Results	Better appreciation for **GPs**
	More memories created

Design

Start	With a "**Quick & Easy (Q&E)**" activity
Mix	(In a few) **Family Fun (FF)** activities
	For bolder **GPs** - pick **Teamwork (TW)** with both playing with the kids

Before GPs come over

Make	Agreement
	To really play nice
	Go a little slower for **GPs**
	Be just a bit quieter
	Help teach **GPs** how to play

Decide   On activities for **GPs**

#2 Hug Me

#6 Hair We Go

#54 Twilight Trip

#57 Pillow Talk

#32 Kitchen Wonders

#34 Mine, Yours, Ours

#16 Praising

#72 Teach Me, Too

#75 Music Tales

#49 Kid Korrection

#98 Park It

#84 See My World

#85 Get the Point

NOTE: **I do not suggest trying "60 Second Scream"**

Concept Origination

Does age difference connect or disconnect?

One of my favorite things, in addition to playing with kids is to bring smiles to the faces of the elderly.

No matter how many aches or pains a person has, when love is provided, pains go away & are replaced with fun new love aches & memories. I began to remember what it was like to be that age again when life was simple, with more trust & happiness.

Keeps Grandparents in the game & on the team.

#30 Caring Catch Up – PF

**They do not know you care until you
take "the time" to care**

Ages	6+
Use	After you are sure about your new partner
	ONE or TWO times a week
	Midweek so it doesn't interfere with the weekend stuff
Benefits	Your partner learns:
	What the little ones think about
	What really matters to them
	Their feelings
	About their past experiences
	Their fears
	Their concerns (even about your relationship)
	Their wants & needs
	Partner becomes accepted & ultimately, bonds with them
You:	See & feel if your partner & kids are right for each other
Materials	Time & patience for you/your partner & your children
Tidbits	Use only with partner that you are confident about
	Be a coach to both your kids & partner

Results   Bonding may not happen over night

They will be more accepting of your partner the more you allow your loving relationship to be seen.

Design

Have   Conversations with your partner prior to using any of the activities

Discuss   Expectations & desires for each of you relating to your children before he (or she) becomes part of the family

Be   Consistent once you get started, to get on the same page

Help them   Set agenda for talks during early weeks

Make   Sure that the little ones are comfortable at all times.

Be   With them as a safety, guiding & calming factor.

NOTE: **There will always be an amount of risk**

There may never be the perfect time

Since this person is not a mom or dad, there will be some level of resistance

In the beginning, you, may have to set early topics

Sample topics:

Food preferences

Favorite school subjects

Fun places they have gone

Friends' names

Fun memories

Sad memories

Activities they did today

Favorite books

Favorite animal

Favorite color

Activities that they like to do:

Alone

W/Siblings

W/Mom (&/or Dad)

W/GPs

W/friends, etc.

The topics are endless!

NOTE: **Do not rush it**

As trust & confidence are built more complex issues can be discussed.

Partner will get to know them at the speed that is comfortable for all of you

It takes time, patience & willingness for everyone: to develop trust & friendship

Watch For any signs of discomfort or change in behavior

If any mild changes occur, slow down

If they are more severe stop, talk to both of them & your partner before continuing

They will always be looking at you for "YOUR" signs of acceptance

If the comfort level does not decrease after NINE to TWELVE months, then realize it may not

Sadly, a personal relationship with this potential partner may not be possible

Concept Origination

Could kids adapt better if we took more time to get acquainted?

A statistic stood out that helped me to create this activity.

Most second marriages break up because of kid challenges.

I don't think that needs to be the case. There must be time invested to truly get to know one another & by setting specific ground rules for all concerned.

I was very interested in learning as much as I could about my girlfriend's kids because they would always be there one way or the other, hopefully, laughter & love would both grow. I quickly realized that when I dated mom, I almost was dating them too.

They appreciate me taking an interest in what they like & think. I know because they still want to play with me!

NOTE: **Allies not enemies**

#31 Separate X Love

For the love of them

Ages	All
Use	After any anger from divorce has subsided & two times/week thereafter to check in for every THREE to SIX months
Benefits	Reassures children of your love even though parents have separate lives
	Gives them stability & keeps focus on them
	Gets both parents on same page of what is best for kids
Materials	Consistency & objective long-term friend to help keep you on track
Tidbits	Do not try to hurt former spouse
	Make 100% agreement between parents to work together for kids benefit
	Phone conversations with them should support other parent's decisions to provide consistency
	No using them to get back at X
Results	They learn that they are not the cause of the divorce
	Less stress & upsets for all
Design	It is for them one of the most important activities you can do for them.
Create	A calming environment in both houses to assure that there will be familiarity for them.

Each parent must support the other as much as possible even though they are not raising them together.

Maintain   Similar bedtimes, eating schedules, food types, etc. as best as you can between households.

Reinforce   Good things about your former partner to them.

Forget blame – that was then, this is now.

Let go   Of need for total control.

Seek   Outside impartial help when you don't agree.

Regularly sit down with **the LITTLE ONES** (or during "**Talkus**") when problems are small.

Bring your "X" on the phone, too, to get a consensus

Saves you time & heartaches by working together for their behalf when at all possible

It also **"nips it in the bud**" any thoughts they may have of pitting you against "X."

As **"Parent Team"** working together there will be assured less conflict, upsets, or stress.

Show you are committed to their happiness

Explain   How your living separate lives will be better for them

Concept Origination

Can parenting be easier after divorce?

This was needed because I have heard that 50% of marriages end in divorce. Many kids believe that divorce is partly their fault. I thought it was time for the parents to reinforce the fact that it is not.

Two people can be in conflict but there is no need to cause kids any more upset. It even reduces the "back in forth" challenges that result even from so called "good divorces."

NOTE: **Two teams can have the same goal**

#32 Kitchen Wonders (KW) – PF

Ages	7+
Use	You want them to safely help in the kitchen
Benefits	Teaches safety & they also learn how to help in the kitchen at an early age
Materials	Kitchen appliances
	Kitchen appliances name chart
	Peel & stick stickers (could be stars or fun smiley faces)
Tidbits	The kitchen can be a place for a lot of mess & noise
	It is a mystery place where mom (most likely) spends a lot of time
Results	They (**the Little & Big ones**) will help you in the kitchen while you cook as soon as they are familiar through learning "**Kitchen Wonders**"
Design	
Explain	That both Boys & Girls can cook. It's fun & healthy
Pull out	A few of the **KWs**: one at a time
	(they can be either magical or scary to them)
Give	Each **KW** a name such as
	Betty the Blender
	Tim the Toaster
	Mickie the Microwave

Deedee the Dishwasher, etc.

Make   Kitchen Wonder FOUR column chart

#1 column – **name KW**

#2 column – Knows **what KW does** (mixes, toasts, etc.)

#3 column – **Who can safely operate KW first**

#4 column – Who can clean **KW**

Place   List on refrigerator

Show   What each **KW** does – then they must identify (**i.e.. Mickie the Microwave** makes food hot, clean with soapy sponge wipe clean with dry towel)

Check off   Column (sticker or initial) when they learn the following:

How each utensil is named

How to safely use each

How they can burn you when hot

How they can cut you, etc.

How to clean it

Give them Twenty-five points for mastering (from the **Points Game)** – points to a prize (like watching a special movie, or use **KWs** to make something fun to eat together)

Make   An agreement to not touch any of the **KWs** without your permission or without you being there with them until TEN.

NOTE: **Keep it very simple – do one at a time until they master their usage – making salads & desserts count too.**

They may not become Martha Stewart, but they will get a good start

Concept Origination

Why do some men & women cook while others do not? Why do some enjoy the creativity & calmness from cooking while others see cooking just as unavoidable?

How could I add more to the former while helping them be safe in the kitchen?

I know why & how now see the therapeutic value or ease of kitchen creations. I

Learned how dangerous the kitchen can be creating burns & cuts, especially for children.

So I decided why not have them help cook in the kitchen & at the same time learn about safety too. Like turning the handle inward so that it cannot be bumped to burn you, wearing potholders to move pots & pans, etc.

Amazingly, I tried it with adults first & then with a few children of different ages ranging from SIX to TEN. Once they felt comfortable in the kitchen, they regularly prepared simple dishes on their own.

They even cooked their mother a special breakfast & dinner. The bottom-line results were they became more involved in shopping, preparing, cooking & even cleaning up after the meals. They became givers not just takers & they gave from their hearts as well.

NOTE: **Simply start by boiling some water together**

#33 Mom's/Dad's Work

Let them know about you at work.

Ages 8+

Use Often while working at home & as a mini family break

Benefits Helps kids understand what you do for work

They become your "Work Ally"

They learn by seeing you work in your job, your career or your passion

Materials Your patience

Tidbits Take the time to explain:

What you do at work (to their understanding)

Why you do what you do

What you like about it

What you must do that you sometimes do not like (travel away)

Help children to understand what parents do at work & what they do not do at work.

Children don't know why parents work late instead of being home with family

Children feel the effect of parents not really being there whether parent is working at the office, on the road, or in the house

Results They see passion, sometimes sacrifice & work go together

Design	Make regular times to share with them what it is you actually do & why
	Help them to become a "work ally" when you really "have to work"
	Now you will get more work done in less time because of their support
	Share simple explanations of your tasks/Share about TEN to FIFTEEN minutes at a time
Tell them	You work because you love them
	It provides for the family
	It makes you happy
	It makes you smarter
NOTE:	**Be totally focused on them for the entire time**
	It will be a pleasant break for you
	Use "Signals" as an invitation for them to come in at the end of each sharing give them "Kisshugs."
Include	The times when you have to take a call in the middle of being with them
	Once they are on your side, they will cause many less interruptions. You will be better at your work & a less stressed parent

#34 Mine, Yours, Ours

They create it, they own it, all celebrate it

Ages	6+
Use	Beginning of each school year & sports season
	Then the middle of each
Benefits	Helps them set their own levels of accomplishments
Materials	Your patience, time, flexibility & a chart to mark their progress
Tidbits	
Make	The first season goal is just to have fun.
Give	Only loving support.
Keep	Fun as a foundation for all activities, not stress.
Ask	A lot of questions so that they own the goals.
Be careful	Not to project your needs over theirs.
Build upon	Effort, agreements, commitment & completion.
Results	They learn by your examples
Design	**First season:**
Tell them	To just have fun
	You also want commitment
	To get to practice on time & learn the rules
Express	Your unconditional love for them for doing & not just winning
Discuss	Activity choices

Value of 100% effort

Joy of participating

What to do if they win - **Celebrate**

What to do if they do not win – Still celebrate but reflect too

Remember the fun you had at their age (how you celebrated what your coach said, lesson learned good & bad times)

Second Season:

Recap	Their achievements from first year or how much fun they had
	(Now that you're bigger, stronger, smarter & know all the rules)
	What did they like best?
	What did they like least?
	Check interest & fun level (for undue stress, fear, dislike, etc.)
	If they are still excited to participate
Determine	Their new goals
Ask	Then agree to the commitment to them – shake on it
	How will they know when they are on track & when not?
	How you can or cannot help, when asked or not asked
	What are their agreed upon rewards from you?

What to do if they get off the mark?

Agree On commitment

Listen To what you say

Eat Healthy with fun foods put in as rewards

Go To bed on time (for older than eight add a little input to agreement)

Do Their chores

(for older than eight add rewards & consequences

Stay With it to get what they want

(Explain what persistence means)

NOTE: **Show how you also set goals to get what you want**

#35 Tag Team - PB & PF

Tag, you are it again & again

Ages	All
Use	At least TWO times week
Benefits	Gives partner an extra hour of sleep
Materials	Great partner
Tidbits	**"Early Bird" - EB -** Partner who gets them up
	"Sleeper Parent or Partner" – SP - Partner who gets to sleep in
	Have them shower the night before & maybe sleep in tomorrow's clothes
Results	**"Sleeper P"** much more refreshed with no kid stuff to do
	"Early Bird" & kids bond then feel good about contribution
Design	**"Early Bird" (EB) & "Sleeper P" (SP)** reverse roles once a week
	"EB" gets them up & does all the parenting stuff without asking for **"SP"** help
	"EB":
	Gets up quietly (part of the fun) – play the **Quiet Game** too
Encourage	Children to remember what they see while out later share

Take   Children to the park, for a breakfast, etc. then to school or back home

"Sleeper P":

Sleep for another blissful undisturbed hour.

Later kids tell SP about special morning surprises during **"Family Matters"**

Concept Origination

It works in wrestling so why not in parenting?

I involve both parents, because I figure the energy level of a kid was comparable to that of two adults.

So instead of one parent becoming worn, frustrated & exhausted, both parents got involved. By passing off them to the other the "fresh" parent keeps things more organized.

NOTE: **Be ready to be tagged & be it**

#36 Come on Over

Share the joy of giving

Ages	6+
Use	At least once a year to clean out unneeded or unused toys
Benefits	Gets rid of toys that they don't use anymore
	Teaches value & making choices
	Teaches sharing
Materials	All their toys, a few friends, wrapping paper, name tags
Tidbits	Let them decide & double check their choices with them
Results	Less toy build up & they learn about giving
Design	They go into their closets, place their toys separate toys into two piles
Keep	Pile ONE Toys
Give	Away toys (to kids without)
	No longer used
	No longer liked
	They are too old for them
	They're slightly broken
	They put all **"Keep Toys"** away

Pick out   At least three toys to give away

They wrap pile TWO

The three **"Give Away Toys."**

They write   A note on the tag that comes from their heart to imagine

How happy the child will be receiving it

Go online   With them & find a local charity that they agree to give the toys for charity

Call   A charity & ask if your children can personally give the toys

NOTE: **Go ASAP then ask how they feel about giving**

#37 Heaven Yes

No one ever really dies as long as they are remembered

Ages	7+
Use	When someone or something close to the child dies
	After a grieving period has passed for **"Loss"**
	When there is a mood change
	If behavior problems arise
	If other signs of pent-up grief appear
	On the lost one's birthday
	As long as your kids are interested
Benefits	Keeps memory of someone or something important in their life
	Keeps them from going into an emotional hole
	Vents pent up sad emotions
Materials	Pictures or objects of the one who is gone
Tidbits	Acknowledge the loss
	Talk about the need to carry on
	Take meaningful length of time to stop, listen & talk
	Continue as long as needed when sadness appears

Results   Openness understanding of regularly & naturally sharing feelings

Life's challenges will come at you & them

Face the sadness of losing someone or something instead of ignoring it

Design

Talk   About how it hurts (you too)

Why it happened

How they can keep their spirit alive

What the person or pet meant to them

What will they miss most

How lost one can still be remembered

Directly to their lost one

Imagine what they may say to them from above.

Say   As long as Lost One Lives in Their Heart Then They Stay Alive

#38 Space Time - PB/ST & PF

A precious gift, the gift of time

Ages	All
Use	When nothing else works - alone time = best medicine
	Life overwhelms you
Benefits	Gives a parent alone time when it is really needed
Materials	Your partner, family or friend comes in as **"Support" (S)**
	At least 4 hours (preferably overnight)
	Best for 24 hours **(FB)**
Tidbits	No need to tell children why & do not feel guilty
Results	Less stressed happier & healthier parent
Design	
Take	Time to decompress when stress or obligations have made it impossible to be with them.
	Call "**S**"
	Say
	You need **"Space Time" (ST)** for 4 to 24 hours
	"S" will understand how important it is
	"S" only asks when & for how long
	"S" comes as soon as possible to get children
	Kids will be told just that they are getting a fun night

NOTE: "**S**" keeps them for the required time

Give **S** a few suggestions to use from this book

Short (FOUR hours)

Take kids to a movie, a meal, a park, etc.

Full Break (FB) (TWENTY-FOUR hours)

"**S**" has them for a sleep over

Now take care of yourself

Take a bath!

Have a drink!

Read

Get nails, hair, etc. done!

Order in or go out

Let Your time be free flowing (you don't need more stress)

It is not a pity party but a time to recharge & relax

VARIATION: W/Partner

You go to a local hotel & let your "**S**" stay at your house.

Let "**S**" checks in with you at certain time

(but not kids - it is 100% about you)

Relax & forget

> The day

> Tomorrow you will be recharged

> You will look forward to seeing them again

NOTE: **The results "WILL" help the whole family**

Concept Origination

> How can moms get a break when it all becomes too much?

> Per the radio news casts, every year, mothers lose it with her kids sometimes with dire consequences. This helps both mom & kids. Moms must have an opportunity to just chill to get away from the situation when nothing else works.

NOTE: **Little space goes a long way**

#39 Time 2 Talk

The "Subjects" Matter

Ages   7+

Use   When "Life's reality" appears at your door or at the dinner table

YOU want to control the way & the timing of "life lessons"

To avoid miscommunication, misinformation, unnecessary fears or confusion

Benefits   Introduces important "life reality" subjects to your kids prior to: Society, TV, School, Friends, Family, or Even Strangers doing it.

Materials   Your simple direct honesty

At least 4 hours (preferably overnight)

Best for 24 hours **(FB)**

Tidbits   Be honest

Most subjects will come at unexpected or unplanned times; That's Life!

Since you cannot always control **"WHEN,"** you need to control **"HOW"**

When the questions arise on others time, do not retreat, move forward with sensible & loving discussions.

Results   You are the source, not society

Design   Don't allow others determine how & when your children learn about subjects such as: sex, death, violence, "bad" people, etc.

Sometimes props can be unbelievably valuable to help talk in the ways they understand

Use   **"Get the Point"** as a way to be sure they understand&.

Give   Them points to explain to you what you just told them

Answer   ALL their questions (if you don't someone else will)

NOTE: **From this time onward, they will not be as innocent as they were before.**

They will be better prepared with the right information than they would be without your input.

If the subject matter is too tough for you to tackle alone, bring in your spouse, family, or trusted friend.

Incorporate Comfort phrases such as:

"I'm telling you this because I love you."

"I would never let anyone hurt you."

Keep   The discussions are as light as possible.

#40 Talkus

**There never is really a dull day,
"Something happens each day"**

Ages	All
Use	At regular times TWO to THREE times a week right after dinner & wind down times
Benefits	Kids always know that they can always talk with their parents no matter what the subject
Materials	Something dedicated to being a **"Talkus"** (a colorful unbreakable object at least twelve inches tall)
	Note pad with each person's name & date
	Typed sheet with general subjects (additional subjects can be added)
	Parent to scribe brief answers
Tidbits	Share with those who care
	Honesty is necessary
	Really listen everyone is quiet while sharing happens
	Display **"Talkus"** in the living room where it is easily seen
	"Talker" is the person sharing
	You'll have to support the littlest ones, but they will get the hang of it very soon
Results	Everyone will be more observant & willing to share their experiences & observations

Design   **You start "Talkus"** signifies what happened today that either Touched someone's feelings or their five senses

Everyone sits at the dinner table to join in

Each person has 1 minute to talk about their day

They talk about something that they noticed today from typed list

Examples: Something they saw

Something that made them happy

Something that made them sad

Something that they ate & how it tasted

Something they touched

Something they heard

An unfamiliar word they learned

Something they smelled

Where they heard the first bird of the day

What the sun, rain, wind, or snow felt like on their skin

After "**Talker**" finishes others

Ask two questions about "**share**" for more details

Once the two questions are answered then they pass "**Talkus**" to the next "**Talker**"

This continues until everyone has two turns.

If someone has something else to share, they can ask for one more turn.

Absolutes: There is something new everyday

Encourage them

To write their experiences every day

Even the dullest day will be more fun when everyone expresses experiences of parts of the same day

Everyone will get better & better at telling stories

Great to share past experiences when someone is feeling down or is sick

#41 Impressions

Stack the Deck to Protect

Ages	6+
Use	Every couple of months
	If any change in their: behavior, sleeping habits or moods
	When new people come into or leave their lives
Benefits	Learn if there are strangers in your child's life in a timely manner
Materials	**THREE by FIVE** cards
	Pad of **EIGHT by ELEVEN** paper
	Crayons for each child
	Print out examples of "emotion" faces from computer on one sheet
Tidbits	Don't react in front of them if something surprises you
	Important that the children feel free to talk without fear of saying something wrong about someone
	Make notes & Follow up
Results	You know things quicker before something inappropriate happens
Design	
Write	The names of a dozen people you know they know on three-by-five cards.
	"Mystery Person" ("MP") at the top of two

"Mystery Person" = any adult that they are exposed to babysitter, your relatives, playmates, playmates parents, teachers, school friends, or even people they may know that you don't.

Tell them To fill in the name (don't push if there isn't any **"Mystery Person"**).

Make Another set of cards with emotional words such as: Happy, Sad, Mean, Nice, Friendly, Loving, Helpful, Scary, etc.

Place Cut out emotion faces in a pile

Show them The card with a name for each person you know

Have them Pick a card with the words that describe their feelings for that person

Place Emotion words to the (person name) card

Example: Grandma = love = face with heart

Brother = smiley face

Sister = sad face

Discuss Their feelings for that person

Do the same for the **"Mystery Person"**

If there is a name or a feeling

Ask Questions to find out more about this person

Keep it in the context of a game, trust must be maintained

#42 Boundaries

Boundaries = give & get respect

Ages	6+
Use	They lose respect for each other, for others or for you
Benefits	Establishes acceptable & unacceptable boundaries
	Teaches respect for one another
Materials	Your will power
	Voice recorder
	Your partner
	Siblings
Tidbits	Fairness is not the key - sensibility is
	Be strong & consistent not harsh
	Be open-minded to everyone's input.
	Set levels of expectations.
Results	Better & more civil communication between siblings
Design	If there is a loss of respect during conversations tape record them
Listen	To what & how things are said.
Ask	Friend to listen & provide suggestions.
	When their conversations sound harsh towards each other use **"What I Want"** to show better examples.

Example:

Give me that!	= **Harsh**
May I please have that?	= **Respectful**
I hate you!	= **Harsh**
I do not understand you	= **Respectful**

NOTE: **Record how "you" talk to them**

We all can become blind or deaf to our own communication style

VARATION: Play tape during **"Family Matters"**

Discuss What feelings came up during conversations or fights.

Say How it hurts your feelings

Ask Do you like being talked to in that way?

Do they talk to their favorite teacher in the same tone?

How do they think the conversation could have gone better?

How good does it make you feel?

Give Rewards when there are positive changes

More time for reading or playing, etc. Or take rewards away

NOTE: **You will not catch all the bad behavior from each one (Sometimes that isn't fair)**

Fairness is not the goal, better conversation is the goal

Their behavior decides on the rewards but are controlled by you.

#43 Hard As

Hard as or Fun as You Make It

Ages 6+

Use You notice them stating how things are **"Hard."**

If they are stopped from finding their own solution.

Benefits Recognizes the difference between tasks that are beyond their capabilities & tasks that are not

Puts definition of **"Hard"** into proper perspective

Identifies obstacles as sometimes good

They learn to ask for help but still do the work

Teaches how to ask for help outside of home

Materials Your lead & help

Tidbits The word **"Hard"** is used too often to describe things that are not, it begins to program the mind.

It takes away possibilities for easy solutions to regular challenges

Notice how often they give up by declaring something too **"Hard."**

When you begin to hear that word regularly, step back from the situation.

Decide if it can be worked out together & not be hard.

Most things can be understood with different approaches, persistence or with help

Results   The word "**Hard**" is put into proper perspective

Design

Teach them To ask but with the intention of them doing the work.

Give   Your definition of what "**Hard**" (really is & is not)

Before you clean = hard

Once you learned it = not hard

Example: "**Hard**" by yourself VS "**Hard**" with someone else's help

Ask   Why it is hard?

Give   FOUR choices

#1 It is too hard to even try

#2 I tried & can't do it

#3 I tried & cannot do it yet

#4 Hard things are more than to learn when you conquer them

If #1   Just try with you there, if they try alone & cannot Congratulate them for trying

If #2   Remind them of tasks that they have already learned that seemed hard once but are now easy to do (brush teeth and ride a bike age appropriate)

If #3   Say that you will help them

Give some examples how others helped you

Explain to them how to overcome something with help & that being hard can be incredibly good too

Next time they come to you & say that something is hard

Ask Why do they think that it is hard?

Have they tried to do it?

How have you tried?

Remind them Of their past successes

Give them Clues to figure the solution

Ask them To give you FOUR possible answers

Tell them To come to you before they say that challenges are "**Hard**" & you both will make it easy.

NOTE: **Do not just give up & do it for them**

Don't just let them give up, they will feel much better for getting the answer

It's ok sometimes to put the "**Hard**" things off to another day (use "**Dove Tail**") – like in the morning

If they notice others saying something is hard that they receive points **(Point Game)**

Concept Origination

Could "**Hard**" be outdated?

"**Hard**" is the second most disliked word I know.

The first word is "**Hate**" - The third word is "**Can't**"

What would the world be like if kids were only given a certain number of times that these words could be used?

Would life be a lot easier? I do not now but am willing to find out.

NOTE: **It is ok to take negative words out of mouth & mind**

#44 Doctor Buddy

Tell the truth, sometimes it does hurt

Ages	All
Use	Before they need to see a doctor/dentist to get a shot
Benefits	Diminishes fear of doctors/dentists & makes appointments go much easier
Materials	Your fingernails
Tidbits	Be honest & tell them that the doctor is there to help
	Many adult fears relating to doctors unnecessarily begin at a young age.
	Most are needless fears that could have been avoided
Results	No more fear of getting shots, giving blood or going to regular check-ups

Design

Use	Honesty when getting a shot
	That it is to make them feel better
Tell them	It feels like a pinch
	That it will only hurt for a moment
	Then pinch them hard on their arm
Tell them	That's all there is
Share	That you feel the same thing

Give them Fifty points **(Point Game)** for being a **"Big"** Boy or Girl for not being afraid of **"Doctor "Buddy"** who wears a coat like a superhero wears his costume - It means that they are good guys to make the bad feelings go away

NOTE: **I effectively used this method while I was in the Army & worked in a medical laboratory**

Concept Origination

Could going to the doctor not cause terror?

I "hate," I do use the word once in a while when it is warranted. This time it is. I "hate" it when parents use police & doctors to scare kids – that is just wrong!

I used to work in a medical lab & one thing I learned was never to lie to a kid. Before, I ever stuck a needle into any little one's arm, I pinched them really hard & told them that that is what it would feel like. Not once after I did that has no kid ever caused me grief or hurt themselves by pulling away at the last minute.

It avoided a lot of tears bruising screams or re-sticks

Ever wonder why many adults have a problem with doctors? Somebody scared them!

Kids are good in most every situation as long as we trust them to be. There's no need to put unnecessary fear into them. I have often heard parents say "if you're not good I'll have a police officer or doctor come & get you.

I also wanted the opportunity for doctors to be nicer too. They generally are nicer when they are not portrayed as villains.

NOTE: **If my dog is not afraid of the veterinarian than my child should not be afraid of the doctor be either**

#45 Kid Power

Start them early as a team not arrivals for life

Ages	7+
Use	Often
Benefits	You get a break & they have fewer fights
Materials	String or rubber bands & stopwatch or watch with second hand
Tidbits	You encourage & support
	Embrace natural competition
	With single child enroll cousins or friends
Results	They do more things together
Design	**"Kid Power" (KP)** - working or playing together to make all tasks easier, better, more fun, etc.
Give them	A project to do together

Project ideas

> Putting away their things
>
> Making bed
>
> Helping with a meal
>
> Helping with **"Music Tales"**
>
> Playing together, etc.

Why: "KP"	Helps them when they work together is more fun
	Gets more done

TWO kids using "**KP**" is better than not using

It takes less time using "**KP**" to complete a project

Before FIRST project

Show them An example of **"KP"**:

Tie   One piece of thread (or rubber band) to the middle of metal bar

Tie   The other end to a fixed object like a doorknob, fence post, etc.

         Have one child pull the metal bar until they break the string (it's easy)

Now tie FIVE pieces of string onto bar pull till it breaks

Add   Additional pieces until 1 person cannot break the string alone.

         Once limit is reached for one, have two kids pull together (string breaks)

Add   As many strings until both of them can't break

Count   The number of strings they can break together

Using chores:

Mess up Each of their beds

Have them make

         Their beds separately

Time them How long it takes until each finishes alone (your energy will be important)

Mess   Their beds up, again

Show them How to work together to make a bed

Time them   Again, until finished while working together

(it should be must faster, especially with your added high energy encouragement)

Say   That's **"KP"**

It works on all the projects they work together on

Encourage them

To use **"KP"** whenever they get stuck, need help or want to work on a project together or when something seems **HARD**

#46 Clean Up - ST

Have fun not fights

Ages   5+

Use   You (really) want them to clean up their mess before company comes

Benefits   Gets them to do it & be excited about it.

Materials   Energy

Tidbits   Progress not perfection

Results   They will **"Clean Up"** a lot when you keep the fun in it.

Design

Create   Urgency for picking up toys, clearing the table, etc.

Your energy will dictate success.

The more energy, the more fun they will have

The more willingness they will have to play

Go over-board, cheer them on!

Challenge them

To finish the task within count of thirty

Count aloud Sometimes slow, sometimes fast (watch reactions)

Creating a sense of urgency always keeps them moving

Be ready to intervene if they try something unsafe

You will be amazed how quickly they speed up the cleanup process

#47 Master Rules - PF

**Master says: "It is not who wins,
it's how you play this game."**

Ages   5 - 8

Use   With different aged groups

Benefits   Diminishes frustrations between older ("**Bigs**")
& younger ("**Littles**")

Play - without conflict

Builds trust

Kids of different ages can play together

Keeps them occupied while you need them to
be occupied

Materials Football, volleyball set, kickball etc.

(Or any group game that can be easily used)

Your high energy

Tidbits   Allow the younger kids to play against the older
ones.

For groups up to ten kids

Master should change rules as soon as
arguments begin say this is how it goes now –
Bigs do this & **Littles** do this

Results   Releases lots of energy, laughter & stops
fighting

Different age groups can play well together

Design

Choose	A known activity such as touch football
Change	Name to **"Whacky Football"**
Play	Like touch football game but create some reasons to give additional points (at any time during the game)
Give	Any number of points to either team **JUST BECAUSE**

With the shortest player

With the longest hair

The biggest smile

The loudest team, etc. (nonsensical reasons)

Make the score outrageously high for each team.

Allow	The older children win.
Keep	The game time limit to an hour
Change	The rules often keep the **"Bigs"** interested.

When you see it in the **"Bigs"** faces that they are getting frustrated & bored.

Give	Extra points for whatever reason you can think of
Call	**Out any score you like (but make it close like 555 – 530)**

They do not really care, as long as the **"Bigs"** win

(**"Littles"** *don't expect to win, they just want to play*)

NOTE: **Do not worry about accurate score keeping**

Let Everyone scores often

No one can argue the score **"The "Master Rules"**

The **"Master Rules"** makes it work, keeps everyone interested & trying

Without **"Master Rules"** the **"Bigs"** don't want to play with the "Littles" since they do not understand& the regular rules & are too easy to beat

They will want to play **"Whacky Football"** again & again

Do not be surprised if the neighbor kids knock on your door to play (it happened to me)

Email me if you have a problem creating "Master Rules" for other team games

Concept Origination

Kids of different ages seemed to always argue while playing.

Was there a way that kids of different ages could play without fighting?

This came from playing with my nephews, nieces & their friends.

Under normal circumstances when they played, there was considerable fighting about rules. Most of the time, I just played referee. I constantly heard "he did this" & "she did this," etc. it was obviously no fun for me.

Since, I had the responsibility & was spending my time with them. I knew that someone had to take charge. I decided that it was going to be me! I told them **"I AM THE GAME MASTER & I MAKE ALL THE RULES."** I mean what did they know, I was bigger & older. They luckily did not ask questions.

From then on, if a dispute came up in a game they were playing, I simply changed the rules. I even changed the name of the game or combined a few together. It drove them crazy but at the same time, it kept them so of guard that it solved 99% of former problems.

No need to try to please everyone with one set of rules, the big guys always won but everyone scored & definitely had fun. The proof came in the form of other kids showing up to play based on what they had heard from their little friends.

NOTE: **Rules are in the hands of the Master**

#48 Stand on Your Head

We must grow old – yes, but we don't have to grow up

Ages	All
Use	Nothing else works
Benefits	Shows your kids that you have had enough
	You stay sane in an outrageous way without taking it out on them
Materials	Pillow, comfortable workout clothes & sense of humor
Tidbits	Use when they have gone too far & shock value is needed
Results	They get their shocked & you get their attention
	They will not believe it but know that you mean what you say (don't be surprised if they howl with laughter)
Design	
Imagine	You've been yelling at them
	They do not respond tonight
	None of the activities seem to get their attention
	Before your next yell, stop everything.
Say	if they don't mind you, then you will stand on your head until they do
	Do not say another word
	If they continue, get up, go stand on your head against the wall or *equivalent

NOTE: **While against the wall tune them out**

Do not respond for a few minutes

Your action shows them that you are serious

Do not make empty threats

Most likely, you will only have to do it once to get the desired effect

It is great for shock value & really works

They will even want to join you to stand on their head too

*If standing on your head seems too much be just as outrageous by standing in front on the couch turn, face it, bend towards couch until your head is on the cushion It's basically telling them that - You "Don't Care & Are Not Concerned."

#49 Kid Correction – PF

It is what they do, not them

Ages	6+
Use	They are exposed to things that are not your values
	If they are having behavior problems
Benefits	Overcomes undue influence from others
Materials	Agreed upon penalties
Tidbits	Be consistent, do not threaten
	Take something away a privilege they have – first time for 2 hours, second time in same week – 8 hours & Third time 24 hours to a week (What was agreed upon prior to infraction)
Results	They know what is right
Design	Attitudes, habits, arguments & resistance that are caused by outside influences show up in many different ways, some of which could be:
	Leaving their **"stuff"** everywhere (it should not be)
	Not picking up after themselves
	Arguing when asked to pick up
	Saying bad words
	Inappropriate dress
	Back talking
	Not listening, etc.

Discuss   Why it is bad behavior

Why you do not approve of it

What you will do if they keep up the bad behavior

That you love them but not their behavior

How it makes you feel

What **"Big" Boys** or **"Big" Girls** do & don't do

Privilege

Examples: Staying up later

Going shopping with mom

Choosing a movie to watch

Picking the meal for dinner, etc.

Spending the night over my friends or have friends over for a sleep over

Something that is meaningful to them, but which can be taken away as a punishment

Create   A list of "**Kid Correction**" penalties from a list of 10 privileges they agree to if they have bad behavior or bad attitudes from the **DESIGN LIST** above

NOTE: **When bad behavior shows up: Identify behavior problem - pull out agreement - allow them two choices for their own correction - use it!**

#50 Shelve It – ST

That worth having, is worth waiting for

Ages	6+
Use	They ask you to buy something that doesn't need to be decided on today
	You have had enough of their asking today
Benefits	Teaches them to make choices
Materials	Three reasons - WHY
Tidbits	
Delay	Buying something they **"think"** they want
Make	**"Decision Time"** after lunch the following day
Results	Wheat is separated from the shaft
Design	Decision has to be made after lunch tomorrow
	When they keep bugging you to buy something
	You do not want to decide now to say **"Shelve It"**
	While **"Shelved It"** they must produce three reasons why they want it: reasons can't be just that "other than my friends have it" or "just because"
	Your yes or no answer will be based on their reason
Listen	Carefully, if they have **"pretty good"** reason, give in & say yes.
	If they have a bad reason, no reason or no effort put into a reason say: no (argument allowed)

#51 Do It, It's Fun

Ya gotta do what ya gotta do

Ages	5+
Use	ONCE a month or TWO or THREE times a month after age 7
Benefits	Increases their responsibility level
Materials	Your teaching cap
Tidbits	Be consistent
	It's like doing homework, playing or both
Results	They learn to have fun doing mundane tasks

Design

Set	Doable chores for them to do
Present	Chores in a fun way
Check	Their results
Show Them	Chores that they can help do such as laundry, watering plants, picking up leaves, etc.

Set

Example	Choose to have fun by doing chores in a fun way
	(Playing music & singing while putting away clothes for example)
Teach	That you can have fun doing **"anything"** even things that don't always seem to be fun even homework (they can listen to music, whistle or even sing during homework or chores

Create   Chore list for: their room – the living room,
             kitchen, bathroom (s)

Reinforce   How nice everything looks when clean

             To be with you when you wash the clothes

Help   You fold the clothes

Talk & share While cleaning

NOTE: **If you have someone doing all your chores,
             have them tag along with them to get an
             understanding of what they do**

             **These are skills that they will use all of their
             lives that may even help them when picking
             a future mate!**

#52 What I Want

Get the "Want" not the "Don't Want"

Ages	6+
Use	Their **"actions"** conflict with your desires
Benefits	Clarifies what you want from them
Materials	Your patience
Tidbits	Pause after conflicting actions;
Express	What you want in a positive statement
Give them	Points when they can repeat the phrase back to you
Then do	What you want them to do instead
Results	Everyone's self-esteem is maintained & better understood **"WHY"**
	Actions change for the better
Design	
Get them	To do what you really want them to do by positive reinforcement not negative discipline.
	How many times do you tell them what you don't want them to do?
Don't	Slam the door
Run	Across the street without stopping & looking
Yell	At your sister (brother)
Leave	Your clothes on the floor
Track	Mud into the house

Talk Back

     (Just a small sample)

Write On a pad the most common "**Don't Do**" statements that you make to them

NOTE: **Though the "Don't Do's" are based on your love & desire for them not to get hurt, etc., they don't know that**

Take Your **"Don't Dos"** from above rephrase them into **"What I Want"**

     I want you to close the door slowly

Stop & watch For cars before crossing street

Speak In a nice way to your sister (brother) because you love them

Pick up Your clothes

Wipe Your feet before coming in the house

Listen To what I say

  It may not always be easy, but put yourself in the place of your child which would you respond better to?

     Now when bad behavior or action arises

     Choose:

     "What I Want" phrase & use one

     Your benefits will make you feel better, too

     Less confusion & conflict for all

     They know what you want them to learn (very quickly)

They learn that you want them to do these things because you love them

Add **"I love you & want you to…."**

NOTE: **You will be surprised how quickly they pick it up**

Communication Category #3
Family Fun

53 My Own Week - PF
Everyone should have at least one

54 Twilight Trip - PB & PF
All quiet on the home front

55 My Parents - PF
I see you in many ways

56 Family Matters - PF
Like nothing else

57 Pillow Talk - PF
Wonderful Whispers

58 My Gifts - PB & PF
From the heart

59 Newbie
Someone new & fun

60 Milestones
Can't be helped

61 Just an Event
It's important to me

62 My Meeting - PF
Just for fun

#53 My Own Week – PF

A new tradition, a week of giving

Ages	5+
Use	Entire week before Birthday Kid's birthday
Benefits	Gives a special week for **Birthday Kid** (**BK**)
	Everyone gives "**Love Gifts**" (**LGs**) to the **BK**
	Every day during the week before birthday
Materials	Love, small bell, imagination & poster board
Tidbits	Good for MULTIPLE SIBLINGS
Results	**BK** feels special, instead of all the emphasis being on the party with friends they will see how much family cares.
Design:	Day ONE thru SIX prior to **BK's** birthday
Get	Large poster board
Place	Picture of **BK** in the middle of a poster board
Write	At the top "In Honor of … Because We Love You."
Then write	"**Love Gifts**" (**LG**) underneath
Have	(A fun) family meeting & ask everyone to commit to do something for **BK** each day of the week prior to the actual birthday. (21 items)

Love Gifts range

FR: Doing the **BK's** normal chores

TO: Putting tooth paste on **BK's** toothbrush

Once list is complete: Everyone signs at the bottom

Present   It to the **BK**

Post   It outside **BKs** bedroom door for all to see

Write   Each **LG** on small piece of paper

Place   It in **Family Matters Bowl**

Each family member draws the number of **LGs** they are going to do then they start doing (mom & dad can help with as many as possible—at least THREE per day

Ring   The bell

Glue piece of paper on chart once completed - each time someone does something for **BK** (so whole family knows an **"LG"** is being given)

It's fun to hear the bell go off many different times

Keep   **BK** involved by having them check off what was done.

Take   A picture of **BK** by completed **LG** poster Board

Day 7

Have   Your typical birthday party

Concept Origination

Can a day of giving turn into a week of giving?

I always wondered why people quit celebrating birthdays. It's not all about presents, it's about gifts!

My definition of a

Present is   **"Something that I want to give you"**

Gift is   **"Something that I give you that you want"**

Birthdays can be something that matters to the whole family

Yes, it is work but it's a **work of love**

NOTE: **Give gifts instead of presents. Gifts can cost nothing too**

#54 Twilight Trip – PF

A revitalization practice, no matter where you are

Ages   6+

Use   When the mood hits you

Minimum once every month or quarterly no matter the weather

When outside stress dictates

Before & after sunset

Benefits   You all enjoy the end of the day for quiet reflection

Be present, focus on clouds, colors, birds the sounds

Materials   Location with unobstructed view, camera, blanket, frisbee, gloves & ball, journal

Tidbits   Recreate anywhere no matter how old you are, where your children are or no matter what is going on in your life

They will instantly connect to it

They will want to play while here

This will last a lifetime as a family connector

Design: Special trip called the **"Twilight Trip"**

They will ask you to take them regularly in the future

Find   A special place for connecting & watching the sunset within a FIFTEEN-minute drive time or even within walking distance from your house for **"Twilight Trips"**

It's important to have a location at a place that is very convenient. A place that doesn't change much such as a park, a hill, a lake or by the ocean

Let them   Go wild, tell them that right before the sun goes down, everyone comes together to hold hands or hug right before as the sun goes down

From time to time bring the camera to capture the moments

The pictures will be great additions to **"Picture Wish" or "Sanctuary"**

Concept Origination

Is there a best time of the day for families to bond?

The time for me has always been right before sunset & the next 10 – 15 minutes after.

Cool air, a beautiful sky like a smile from GOD.

I remember so many times in bygone days when it seemed that the end of the day always ended in our front yard.

We are more crowded but there is still a place for a peaceful time to say goodbye to the day & goodbye to the day as a whole family.

NOTE: **Don't forget to look for the Green flash**

#55 My Parents – PF

**What you think you are, what you are
& how they see you**

Ages   6+

Use   At least once or when you're curious

Benefits   Learn & see how your kids see you

The children take pictures of mom & dad for whole day

Materials   Digital camera

Tidbits   Let them take pictures of you: inside, outside, in the car, at the store etc.

Results   Sometimes **"YOU"** need to see how they see you

Design

Pick   A regular time during the month

Encourage them

To take as many pictures in one day as they can

NOTE: **Make sure they take pictures of you when they're happy seeing you!**

Just go about your normal routine during the day (you'll soon forget about them)

At the end of the day download pictures

Next day after dinner:

Sit with them

Have them pick pictures that they feel look most like you

Mom/mad/happy/sad/silly, etc. same for dad

Don't judge their choices

Don't defend yourself

Just listen

NOTE: **It's important to see yourself when you're not in the best of Moods with them**

You can remember each moment what you were actually thinking

You'll find that many times your face said one thing to them while you may have been thinking something different

Now ask them to pick their favorite three pictures of you

Why these pictures?

They'll get it

They love you

They'll tell & show you

You will be proud of yourself

YOU ARE WONDERFUL PARENTS!

Concept Origination

How do we really look to our kids? (this was created just by accident!)

One day my girlfriend told me about the time, her little five-year-old daughter took mom's digital camera & started taking pictures of "**The Mom**" (as she affectionately referred to her as) throughout the whole day. "**The Mom**" had no idea how she looked through the eyes of her five-year-old.

Some pictures were basic but most revealed how much her daughter loved her. What a nice gift. This is an easy way to see how things are going between you & them without a lot of words.

NOTE: **Try it with them at different ages say on your birthday as a gift to you**

#56 Family Matters – PF

"Family Matters" matter

Ages	All
Use	At least once a week
Benefits	Creates important family unity & traditions
Materials	A **Family Matters** Bowl, three different color sticky pads
	Fun books, board games & card games
Tidbits	The first time you use this, come up with fun ideas to do together (write them down on different color sticky notes)
	Place ideas in jar
	Draw one final idea each week.
	Use **"Get the Point"** at the start to keep them focused
	It's important that the activities be diverse to stimulate conversation
	The goal is to interact as a family
	Trust & family bonding is created when everyone sticks to it
Results	You will become better friends as a family
Design	Entire family creates & plays activities together
	Spend at least 30 minutes for the game
Write	The words **"Family Matters Night"** on a sheet of paper

Put it   On the refrigerator for all to see

Set   **Family Matters** Day

Thursdays work great before weekend madness right after dinner (make dinner easy & quick - say pizza?)

Everyone creates SIX different types of activities based on colors

Chosen (up to TWENTY-FIVE can be picked from this book – write on sticky pad and place in the bowl)

Green = family games

Pink = reading for each other, storytelling, singing (use **"Performance Plus"**)

Blue = family projects, crafts, etc

BONUS: YOU CAN PICK UP TO 30 activities from this book from each of the four categories Place

Ideas in **"Family Matters Bowl"**

NOTE: **You'll see & feel more of a commitment to the family as time goes by**

It teaches each family member to give to each other & put the family as a priority

Everyone at one time or another will challenge the **"Family Matters"** night when there is something else more exciting comes along like friends, work, & events

No matter what else comes up on these nights
"FAMILY COMES FIRST"

Concept Origination

Does the word family still have meaning?

I'm just old fashioned. There used to be time for family. Family used to come first.

In my mind of all the things that come & go, there should be times where nothing else is more important than the family.

I believe that family traditions can still be made & kept, even in this fast-paced crazy lifestyle everyone lives today. Those using "**Family Matters**" learn this too.

NOTE: **Family =**
           FUN
           ALWAYS
           MAKING
           IMPORTANT
           LASTING
           YEARS

#57 Pillow Talk – PF

Easy does it, does it every time

Ages	All
Use	Weekly
	When everyone needs a nap
Benefits	Enjoy the **"NOW"**
Materials	Pillows
	Your undivided attention
Tidbits	You or they can ask for it more often
	If something is bothering them
	Make environment as quiet as possible
Results	**"Pillow Talk"** is both giving & getting
Design	Low light (candles or fireplace)
Lie	On the bed or the floor
	All of you grab a pillow
Lay	On the living room floor (without any unnecessary noise)
Just talk	About whatever or nothing in particular
Go	Wherever the mood takes you
	They can also ask just for dad or you one on one **"Pillow Talk"**

NOTE: **It's OK if everyone falls asleep, in fact it's especially effective too if something is upsetting to them, take a break, right here, right now, do it.**

Concept Origination

Can we still have simple loving conversations?

There was a movie called **"Pillow Talk"** with Rock Hudson & Doris Day. I liked the visual of calm fun talk between the two characters in the movie while lying on their pillows.

I envisioned a time where actual quiet conversations took place. Quiet time with shared talks about everything, a place for kids & parents to lie down together with their heads close together on pillows.

We tried it, they liked it, & it's now in this book!

BONUS: The Bigger the pillow the better

are a Monarch
Butterfly?"

#58 My Gifts – PB & PF

You're born only once, so celebrate!

Ages	5+
Use	3 days before "**Birthday Parent's**" (BP) birthday
Benefits	Gets them involved in parents' birthday
	It will last a lifetime
Materials	Cake mix, party favors, balloons, flowers,
	"Little Ones" homemade banner w/handprints (Happy Birthday written on)
	Camera/video camera
Tidbits	Hype it up
	Non-BP tells them how much **BP** will be surprised **(BP - be surprised!)**
	If you (or dad) are alone bring in **Helper (H)** uncle, aunt or grandparents
	Take lots of pictures
Results	Fun for you & they feel like heroes
Design	I love birthdays
	Kids love birthdays (you can also learn to love yours)
Make	This a real giving time for your kids by teaching them what it means to give (especially to you)

Week prior to party:

> "**H**" invites family & friends to **BP's** party with or without **BPs** knowledge

4 days prior to party:

> "**H**" tells **them**
>
> That they are going to give **BP** gifts, gifts of being good (birthday party)

"H" calls & confirms guest list

> (Explain – that kids will call again as if they're inviting them)

Mark "**Color My Days Calendar**"

"H" & kids decide

> On the gifts

BP gives

"**H**" gift suggestions (without kids knowing)

Gift suggestions:

> They do their chores (happily) on ....
>
> They get up easier on.........morning
>
> They are quiet for ....amount of time
>
> They do not fight for .... amount of time
>
> They clean up.......
>
> When they decide, "**H**" writes down on a colorful chart titled "**My Gifts**" they sign it
>
> **Post** on the refrigerator

THREE days prior to party:

>"H" & kids announce to **BP**

TWO days prior to party:

>As they do the items they shout out:
>
>**My Gift** to you mommy (daddy) is …. (From the chart)

BP makes It a big deal of noticing (makes them feel great)

Day prior to party:

>"H" & kids make decorations, posters, homemade birthday card, gift cards (put under beds to be ready for next day)

Make Cake (if time) or go to bakery (let them pick it out)

>They call **BPs** friends to invite (those who already said yes earlier to **("H")**

Early party day

BP leaves To go on errands (& relax), they decorate

THREE to FOUR hours later

BP returns To a surprise party!

>Everyone eats, drinks & is (very) merry

BP tells Guests about all of the **"Gifts"** they have received

NOTE: **No matter what it is it's very important for "BP" to act surprised!**

Concept Origination

When can kids learn to give from the heart?

I love to surprise people. Kids are so much fun when they get up to something, especially when they are doing it with love.

I have never had a problem encouraging children to create a gift for mom or dad. It is a special time to give a gift of love on mom or dad's birthday.

BONUS: You see things you never would have before

#59 Newbie

Everyone welcomes the newest addition

Ages   All

Use   Early in your pregnancy

Often before a new family addition is added

Benefits   Makes transition smooth for a new child to arrive into the family whether by birth or adoption

Reassures existing child(ren) the benefits the **"Newbie"** brings coming into the family

Materials   First child's scrap books

Tidbits   Continue to give a lot of attention to the existing child

Explain all the fun it will be when the "**Newbie**" arrives

Explain how much you will need their help too

Design   When you are adding to the family, there may be a little confusion as to why there's another child coming into the family

Explain   How "**Newbie**" coming into the family is good for them & everyone else

Encourage them

To ask any questions or fear that they have

Keep   All discussions upbeat

Include them In any **"Newbie"** arrival preparations as soon as possible

Have your partner add their input

Ask   Lots of questions about how they are feeling

Continually tell them

How: Much you love them

Happy that you are able to give them a little brother or sister

Special they are

Pleased that they are going to help you with the **"Newbie"**

The **"Newbie"** is so lucky to have them as a big brother/sister

Also, if adopting share how the **"Newbie"** will feel coming to the family

Obviously, change the word newbie as soon as you have a name for the baby

He (or she) will be looking forward to playing with them & happy they will be to having him for a big brother or sister

Concept Origination

Could sibling or pet rivalry never exist?

I heard many years ago that when babies are brought home & the family dog is pushed away, the dog's resentments build (sometimes) to a dangerous level.

Similar resentments are often unknowingly created between the older & newbie child.

Sometimes these resentments last a lifetime. They don't have to be there in the first place!

The **"Big"** child adapts best to a newbie when they are included into the fold very early in mom's pregnancy. All the good things are discussed with them. Now they look forward to the newbie's arrival. They don't feel that there's an unexplained or unwanted rival appearing.

NOTE: **Buy-in now avoids disasters later**

#60 Milestones

Don't fight them, notice & celebrate them

Ages	6+
Use	Once a month
Benefits	Recognition of the many **milestones** as they grow
	Celebration of benchmarks
Materials	Journal & child growth books
Tidbits	Savor these moments for the future
	(**Milestones** quickly pass never to return)
Results	Notice whether **Milestones** are happening
Design	A chance to slow down
Savor	Their growth process, the time will be gone soon enough
Enjoy	These amazing times
Make	List of "important" of one hundred things that "you" consider childhood **"Milestones"**
Examples:	Hear them say a new word
	They reach a new height
	Their first sleep over
	Their first friend
	The first time they help with the chores
	First time they ride their bike without training wheels

Create	A chart of at least a dozen things can be checked monthly
	You'll notice amazing changes occurring in them
	Bringing changes into awareness will mean more to you later on in life
Example:	For a doctor who is now grownup
	When was the first **MILESTONE** when she showed interest in helping people?
	The first time I walked the old lady across the street when she was 6 years old
Get them	Excited about some of the fun changes they can look forward to
Celebrate	The little things too
NOTE:	**Many of these "Milestones" will mean more to you as the years go by (especially when they have little ones of their own.)**

Concept Origination

Can we capture the moments that really matter?

They grow so fast. I've gone into old houses & seen the marks parents made marking their kids' growth points.

Since so many people don't stay in the same house for many years anymore, I really wanted to make memorable moments last & last as best they could.

BONUS: You notice so many different kinds of milestones now

#61 Just an Event

Sometimes small things mean a lot

Ages	6+
Use	You want them to notice the "little" things
Benefits	There is recognition of events important to **"them"** but could go unnoticed by you
Materials	Colorful calendar (large wall calendar), camera & journal for you & them
Tidbits	Be present
	Take notice of how certain events affect them
	Notice their reaction to certain events
Results	**"Good stuff"** is noticed
Design	They want attention for something that means something to them
Examples:	Dressing themselves for the first time
	Pouring their own cereal
	Tying their shoes
	Putting something away on their own
Tell them	To tell you if something meant something to them that you missed by saying **"Just an Event."**

They tell you

> What it was (don't judge: it meant something to them)

> If you missed it the first time, notice & acknowledge it now (with a hug or kiss)

Write   A line in a either journal &/or write on **"Colorful Days"** Calendar

NOTE: **You too, can have or call "Just an Event"!**

#62 My Meeting – PF

Be with them then let the world revolve around you for a change

Ages	All
Use	They need your closeness or attention day or night
Benefits	World is ignored for a while & lets them be only with you
Materials	TWO (non-see through) bed sheets or quilts & flashlight
Tidbits	Use inside or outside
	Use high energy
	Yes, they will be noisy
	No matter outside activities, focus on what they want to do under the covers (in their meeting)
Results	Magic happens once you're under them (covers)
Design	Fun activity that gives them a voice
	It's great to use one on one or with (up to THREE) others
	Before the start of an outdoor event
Lay	Sheets or quilts out on the ground in a park
	Everyone in your group gets under the covers
	They take turns being in charge

NOTE: **Whatever fun happens, happens**

The key & beauty is that they get to use their imagination

They love feeling special & having you under with them

They also get a kick out of being the center of attention

Encourage them

To be silly & loud

PERSONAL NOTE:

I had a great time during the 4th of July with my girlfriend & her two girls (5 & 7) they ran the show, lots of laughter & screams of delight

#63 Get Down to Color

Cool Creative Colorings

Ages   All

Use   Rainy days & when they don't want to go out or you need a stress reliever

Benefits Embraces the individuality of each child

Materials Blank paper & lots of crayons

Tidbits   Specify a color time, total fun - no color rules, get down there with them

Results   Like no other coloring they've ever done

You all have fun

They learn to trust themselves while having fun

Design   Each of you draws many lines in different directions on plain paper

Then color between each bordered shape

When finished coloring rub paper over a blank page

(it will make the pictures very shinny)

If you use a coloring book

Don't worry about keeping within the lines or the **"right"** colors

Color outside & color characters any color they want

(They truly can make elephants pink if they want)

THEIR CREATIVITY IS THE KEY

Ask them What they are creating

Tell them That there are no rules

Once item colored

Cut out   Shapes & tape them on the walls as decorations

NOTE: **Play up unique creations to visiting GPs, relatives & friends. They will be proud that you make a big thing of it**

Concept Origination

Can kids create outside of the rules?

Once, I gave them permission to give up the **"coloring rules"** – color between the lines, color only certain colors, etc.

I also wanted most of the fun to come after they colored. Inspire them to share their individual (nontraditional color) creations.

They always have an answer. I just listen, ask more questions & smile at their explanations. A benefit was that their creativity started to blossom in other areas as well.

NOTE: **Questions may come regarding other boundaries real or imagined**

#64 Little Campers – PF

**Time with nature, time with you,
is there anything better?**

Ages   6+

Use   Non-school nights & on beautiful summer or spring nights

Benefits   Gives them a camping experience without leaving home

Materials   Sense of adventure

Inside - good pillow & blankets, outdoor or animal sound CD, CD player

Outside - FOUR-person tent, air mattress, sleeping bags, lawn chairs, fire

One **"Camper Parent" (CP)**

One **"Helper Parent" (HP)** for support role

Tidbits   One **CP** sleeps with them either way

Invite   Sleepover friends

Don't worry if you've never camped, call a friend or family member, someone you know is a good camper, ask for tips but above all, have fun with the kids

Kids may never fall asleep

Results   They'll never forget their favorite camp out

Design   Inside during winter, rain or when they're too small for outdoors

Outside with good weather & when they're a bit older

Inside "Camper Parent"

Place blanket over TWO couches works great

Play animal sound CD adds to the fun

Shut all lights out

Have flashlights & a fire in the fireplace is perfect

Roast marshmallows in the fire

(A microwave works if there is no fireplace)

Is there a storyteller in the family? Invite them over

Less mess, less fuss, more fun!

Outside "Camper Parent"

Has them help you to set up tent in back yard

For 8 + year olds bring them to a close campground (set up IS part of the fun)

Make   A fire (bring your own kindling or everyone finds it together

Cook   Hotdogs, etc. smores later

Invite   Other parents to stop by to tell stories

Count   The Stars or the clouds on a full moon

Point   Out Constellations (simple picture books can be found)

"Helper Parent"

Makes sandwiches, cookies & hot chocolate

Takes care of anyone who may get scared or dislikes it

Plays the goffer role (go for this, go for that)

NOTE: **In both cases make one parent sleep with them all night**

#65 Performance Plus – PF

Performance plus Love

Ages	ALL
Use	Quarterly & when they ask you
Benefits	Confidence builder & just plain fun
Materials	Master of ceremonies
	Backstage coach
	Chairs for an audience
	Area separated by a curtain
	Homemade costumes are necessary
	Friends & family audience
	Audience participation
Tidbits	Every kid is naturally a performer
	Help them to spread their wings
	It's the doing not how good they are at encouraging, encourage, encourage - Do not compare – keep it light – do not push
Results	Shyness – Disappears
	Confidence – Appears
Design	FOUR kids or more
Use	Seasonal themes
	At least THREE to FIVE minutes for each performer (enough time for) **"Do Overs"** or just – **"Do it Again"**

TWO acts for each performance

ONE intermission

Create   A **"Performance Plus"** show for - Mom, dad, friends, family & neighbors

A **Master of Ceremonies** (mom or dad – biggest ham) introduces performers

Use   A name that may sound like performance:

Jimmy the Gymnast

Sally the Singer

(You can give a stage name different than their first names)

David the Dare Devil

Tammy the Terror

Anything goes

Performance ideas:

Standing on their head

Doing a split, Kicks

Singing, Jump Rope

Dancing - free style, ballet, partners (mom or dad)

Magic tricks (even as helper)

Gymnastics

Doll Theatre

Reading aloud

Something they learned in school

Etc., etc. there's no limit!

Don't forget audience participation

Mom & dad (**always**) be guinea pig volunteers

These will be very memorable nights for you & especially them

Make   Stage area & sheet curtain

Replace   Red, green & blue light bulbs

Make   Simple costumes (from their closet) or make a quick trip to a Goodwill store (budget no more than $10 per costume

Practice   &   talk   it   up

Backstage coach helps them

Get ready & keep their performance going

It's all good. Keep the fun & energy up

Once they do their bit clap like crazy

I mean like crazy!   The more you give - the more you get!

As they finish, they join the audience

Create: TWO different performances for each

Have intermission for costume changes, cookies & drinks.

Part 2   Reintroduce players

They do their second performance

Everyone gets acknowledged individually & as a group

Concept Origination

How do real entertainers begin?

I've heard that many comedians, actors & singers got their start by performing in front of their family as kids. They got applause. It got them.

I thought why not give "yours" the same good feelings & give them a way to build their confidence. Plus this is a way to get them over being shy (I know what that feels like to be shy & not to be fully expressive. This helps them to become fully expressed in a matter of hours!

BONUS: A star is not born but they can grow

#66 Adventure Workout

**No more reason to miss a workout again,
you will look forward to it.**

Ages 6+

Use You want an outside workout

Benefits You get your workout while they're still with you

Materials **Heart trail** & children's fairytale book

Tidbits Include them during this workout

Results You enjoy them while you work out (no more giving up activity for yourself)

Design

Find A "**Heart Trail**" Workout trail that has the 15 – 20 different exercise stations you stop at as you jog around

Buy A good **fairy tale** book with many characters & a lots of action

Have Them read it aloud to you while you workout

Incorporate "**Fairy tale**" characters into each workout station

You play different characters as you work out or you & your kids act like you're in the story & use the stations as props

Example: Your pushups could equal you looking under a log to find something in the story

Encourage them

> To imagine the story as you do each exercise & to join you doing some of the exercises

> They also do a few pushups while they help you look under the (story log) If they get stuck, then add something from modern life they understand &. (Again, using pushups as an example) as you do your pushups

Tell them   To imagine that they are looking under their bed to find something in the story

> The key is just to do your workout, use imagination & be together

NOTE: **You'll be surprised how fun your workout will be for all of you & you'll even start looking for fun books to act out!**

#67 Pause Because – PF

Home-Life is not Work-Life

Ages   All

Use   Every day after work

Benefits Late coming home spouse gets HALF hr. to be alone before having home challenges

After pause they participate 100% in **"Home Front" (HF)**

Materials **Designated "Home Base" (HB)** – could be tree, fence gate, mailbox, etc. something that when touched is a reminder to leave work outside

Tidbits   Be consistent

Results   More focus on the family & separation from work

Design   Whichever parent gets home from work last will get a THIRTY-minute break before jumping into family business

30 minutes allows last arriving parent to change gears from work mode to true home mode – parent can walk outside alone, take a THIRTY-minute nap, sit in favorite chair, whatever but have THIRTY minutes undisturbed before family crashes in

After the break they must give full attention to the family the good, the bad, the ugly & finally the good again

NOTE: **The needed decompression time will benefit kids too**

30 minutes begins as soon as you touch **"HB"** = A special part of the home, such as a tree, a bench, a fence post

Once **"HB"** is touched, work mode must dissolve & **"HF"** begins

There will be time for work talk in the morning if needed

The night belongs to the family

No matter what happened at home, THIRTY-minute decompression is honored!

Concept Origination

How to be present with home?

How to give up the work life?

How to change gears between the two?

I remember as a kid, when my dad walked in the door from work, he immediately got all the bad news of what happened in the house. He was told who should be disciplined, etc. before even saying hello. He never was able to ease into the home front first.

I wondered how much less stress would have there been in the house, if he could have eased into the **"home situation**?" Years later, I heard about a man who made a ritual of touching a tree in his yard on his way into the house as a way to transition from work mode to home mode. Could this help with home problems & the working spouse?

I decided to try & combine both the needed **"pause"** **& the transition"** time from work mode to home mode.

A **family practice** was born. A practice that now creates more connection for the whole family instead of resentment or confusion.

This idea is even more valuable now that more moms work or there are more single working parents. It's a mini break to shift gears, it works.

I knew it was a winner when I saw him teaching it to others.

NOTE: **Because you need it**

#68 Picture Wishes – PF

Pictures speak a thousand words & a thousand dreams

Ages   6+

Use   Week before going to school

End of the school year

Week before birthday

Benefits   Through pictures they show what makes them feel good

Materials   All types of old or new magazines travel, fashion, kids, national geographic, houses, parenting, (for starters at least 15 – 20)

One poster board for each person

Glue & scissors for each

Something to play fun music

Tidbits   Don't judge pictures - let them pick what they want

Your encouragement helps them to have free expression

Keep a pile of magazines for more fun for future **"Picture Wishes."**

Results   You learn about them & yourself

Design   There are no rules for picture selections

Part 1

Put   The pile of magazines in front of each person

Tell them That they have 15 minutes to tear any picture that they like out of any magazine, but they must take only three from each magazine then put it back & get pictures from another one

If they ask what to tear out tell them they'll know or give them a topic

Topic suggestions:

Words

Phrases

Vacation

Family

Animals

Flowers

Clothes

Men

Women, etc.

Something pretty – to them

Something that is - mean, scary, ugly, safe, expensive, cheap

What love looks like to them, etc.

Tear out Everything fast without thinking at this stage

Pile it In front of them

As time starts running out, turn up the energy

Do A loud count down

Don't worry About being neat

The faster they tear out pictures the better

After 15 minutes, call time!

Stop   Tearing out pictures

Part 2

Crop   Pictures (as they wish) with scissors

Take   About 30 minutes for this part.

Play   Fun kid music

Do not judge or discourage which picture to use

Part 3

Lay   Poster board down for each of you

Lay   The pictures anywhere on poster

Once they are satisfied:

Let them   Begin pasting pictures

Remember,   There are no rules

Words or pictures can go in any direction & overlay each other

Once they're finished:

Ask them   Why they wish for what's in the picture

Tell them   If they really want what is on the poster, they must hang

"Picture Wish" in a place they can see it everyday

NOTE: **Make your own private collage**

Share or just keep it in a special place

You will see your own growth

Concept Origination

If I don't know, I ask

If I don't see, I look harder

If I don't understand what is wanted, I use pictures

Since pictures say a thousand words; I decided to give up a few thousand words for the sake of clarity.

I used a picture board to show past & present wishes. Because of their pictures, I could make some of their wishes into reality for them.

NOTE: **Pictures are real time information**

#69 All Today

Something Happened Today Find out What

Ages   5+

Use   Wednesdays & Fridays or if **"Talkus"** doesn't work

Benefits   They learn to focus on everyday good stuff

Keeps information flowing

Materials   A list of questions to stimulate their thinking about what happened today

Note pad

Some kind of gifts for points given

Tidbits   Keeps them positive, guides them, it builds their awareness & uses their five senses

Results   Helps them become much more aware of their experiences

Design

Catch   Up on things

Get   More information about what's actually going on with your kids in a day than the typical, **"Nothing"** or **"I don't know"** answers

On appointed days after school begin **"ALL Today"** (to get points.)

Create   A twenty-five question **"All Today"** list

Ask   Who, what where, when & why questions as guides to stimulate thinking:

What did they see while driving in the car?

Who was the first person they saw at school?

What was the first thing the teacher said in class?

Wait　　　　For an answer

Really listen,

Go deeper by saying "then what happened" at least two more times

Their recollection will increase after each **"then what happened,"** instead of them saying - **"fine"** or **"nothing"** (even a boring day is interesting)

Have them　Describe to their day using their five senses

Something that they:

Smelled

Heard

Saw

Felt

Tasted

On the way to school

During school &/or on the way home

You can help them at any time by telling the something you experienced

Each child gets to answer two questions that you pick & two that they pick

Get points if they give you a full description (You'll know full description when you hear it)

Be liberal with the points

After each round they write down the points received

Give wide variety of fun rewards

NOTE: **The main objective is to get them to tune into & really express what really happened during the day**

#70 **I'm Here** Do as one of the First

Protect Your Treasures, NOW

DO THIS within 24 hours of Reading!

Ages   All

Use   Regularly (practice)

Benefits   Protects your most precious gift - them

Materials   Flashlights, whistle, red paint & paint brush

Tidbits   Don't be complaisant

May you never say the phrase "if only we would have made a plan."

20/20 hindsight isn't worth a life

We never think that a catastrophe will happen to us it always happens to others

Don't you or yours become another statistic

Before the need arises & it's too late

Do at night & in the day

For every season, rain or shine

Results   You have an automatic safety plan & have an activity for **"life"**

Design

Goal   Get them out of the house in an emergency

To avoid confusion of where the kids are during an emergency

Make	A plan of how to get out of the house in case of an emergency: Fire, Earthquake, Hurricane or Snowstorm
Show	How to get out of window, where the closest door is
Pick	Two locations across the street at the front of the house & in the backyard
Have them	Practice going to those two sites until it becomes automatic
Make	It fun
Time them	& give them a prize
Cheer them	On tell them also what not do
Tell them	Once they are at their **"safety" point**, to yell out **"their name & I'm Here!"**
	To count to THIRTY then call out again, stay where you are until you or a neighbor, policeman or fireman comes to help them
	Not to go back in the house, for any reason
First time:	
Practice	In the day – first to front then to back
Continue	Two times/week for two weeks in the day
Then	Switch
	To nighttime
Place	Flashlights within reach of their beds

After they've fallen asleep:

Practice	Once for each season (especially important in December)
Use	A whistle in the beginning to get them going
Do	It with them - race them or help them to spots
Give them	Points or rewards when they get there the fastest
NOTE:	**If they are on the second floor make adjustments to get down**
	If they smell smoke to get down on floor & crawl until they get out of the house
	No matter how much they complain still practice until it becomes automatic

#71 Neighborhood

**Get to know your neighbor;
It's the "neighborly" thing to do**

Ages   6+

Use   In a new location

If you've never done it (no matter how long you've lived there)

Before sundown

Weekend mornings

Benefits   Builds a relationship with neighbors for fun & safety

Teaches them how to make friends wherever they are

Materials Introduction piece to put in doors to notify neighbors of your intent to walk around the neighborhood to introduce yourselves

Tidbits   Walk the neighborhood regularly

Target 2 streets in front & two in back

Make extra effort for those neighbors on all four sides of your house

Notice, who is in the neighborhood, as you walk around

Stop to talk for a while & get acquainted

Setup emergency plans with neighbors three houses on both sides of your house (get their names, phone number

Take your time

If it's an apartment 3 neighbors on each side and 2 next level above and 2 level below

Results   Safety net & friends are created

Design

Make   A chart with the addresses of the neighbors

Put   Their names on the chart as you meet them

Continue   Until you have met those within two streets in front & behind your house

Don't worry If some you rule out or that some are rentals

The key is to get understanding of who lives in your neighborhood & potentially to make some lasting friends

Learn   About the neighborhood:

Jot down as many interesting facts as you can of the neighborhood on the chart (# of cats, oldest person, most kids, etc.)

Award them Points for getting the most fun facts

When they get all the names that you will have a neighborhood party

NOTE: When you get acquainted with a few neighbors, invite them for a **"Performance Plus"** as an icebreaker & potentially as a regular event

Concept Origination

What happened to the neighborhood?

What happened to being neighbors?

Was being neighborly in a real neighborhood outdated?

It's seemed obvious just driving around neighborhoods that with TV & video games, opportunities for little ones to make close by friends was almost lost.

No…, it doesn't have to be. I confronted a problem head-on (or actually they by the hands). I took the time to explore who lived within walking distance of our front door.

With not much effort, amazing relationships became available. Many people were willing to accept new friends if someone was willing to take the first steps.

It's almost like everyone else was waiting for the first move. New relationships quickly opened up to kids. A benefit was that moms & dads were as eager to make new friends at the same time.

NOTE: **Your or their best friend could be next door or next door to them**

NOTE: **Tell the little ones that they NEVER go into a neighbor's house unless you are with them NO exceptions!**

#72 Teach Me Too

Teaching is Giving & Understanding

Ages	6+
Use	Every couple of weeks during the school year
	Immediately after they learn something in school
	After you've taught them something
	For anything that they want to share
Benefits	Immediate understanding of lessons
Materials	Time
Tidbits	Be the student, ask questions that helps guide them
	Enjoy their growth
	Acknowledge their level of understanding
	Go back & add the parts they miss
	Congratulate them about what they have learned
	You'll notice their natural strengths for communicating
	Make it a habit - set a time two times/week to teach you
Results	You hear what they actually have learned

Design   There are so many things that your kids are learning every day.

"Teach Me Too" they will show you what they have learned from you & from others

Get them

Started by asking them to show or tell you what lesson they learned from you this week

If they don't remember immediately, gently give them a hint

Give   **"MWA Kisses" & 'Kissugs Count'**

Ask   Questions & stay interested

To teach you something that they learned at school

Encourage them

To act out the lessons, show pictures & tell stories

While they are teaching, you may be surprised how their patience for you & your patience for them increases

You'll look forward to their classes

Once they know that they will become a teacher (to you), they will pay more attention to all of their lessons & hone their listening skills

Pay attention

Watch   How (now) they will be (naturally) drawn towards certain school subjects over others

Concept Origination

What do kids really learn?

I'm always amazed at how much kids really know. I thought that if I set the stage for them to really explain back to parents that they would truly learn something. You would have some extra fun hearing them say it in their words.

Another benefit was that they would begin to pay more attention when they were learning their lessons, since they know that they may be asked to teach it to you later on.

NOTE: **Tell me, show me, do it & teach me too**

#73 What's Cooking? - PF

Have it "Our" Way

Ages   9+

Use   Couple of times a week

Benefits   Each family member gets a voice in what's for dinner

Everyone learns to support the whole process

Much less complaining when everyone is involved

Increased interest at least for this one meal

Fewer tantrums about food, less fussy eating

More interest from them at the grocery store

Materials   Relatively quickly to prepare food stuffs

Tidbits   Food combinations don't always have to make sense

Everyone supports to each other's choice

Everyone must eat it

Be flexible; sometimes go to the store

Other times use what is already in the cabinets

Results   More fun at the dinner table

Design

Mark   A calendar on the refrigerator

Everyone plans

> The meal at some level

Everyone writes

> In the calendar what they want on Saturdays

> **FIRST Saturday** - Mom picks main meat, kids the vegetables, dad the dessert

> **SECOND Saturday** - Kids pick main course, dad the vegetables, mom the drinks/dessert

> **THIRD Saturday** – Dad the main course, mom the vegetables, kids' the drinks/dessert

> **FOURTH Saturday** - Kids pick the entire meal

Concept Origination

> If they had a voice, would life be easier at mealtimes?

> Why not, I said to myself! Kids eat what we give them all the time, so why not turn the tables?

> Now parents eat what they want for a change! The combinations that they come up with are never boring. Almost like "kids' revenge" for having to eat their spinach.

> No, it won't kill you.

> You'll even have some fun memories.

> **BONUS: Eating will never be boring again**

#74 Four Memories for Memories - PF

A Meal for their Minds

Ages　　　　5+

Use　　　　As soon as they can read

Benefits　　Stretches their minds without pushing

Expands their memories

Develops their focus

Materials　Ten small toys each a different solid color

Tidbits　　Be aware of any undue stress & back it down if there is any undue frustration

Be patient & build their confidence

Results　　Memory is enhanced

Design

Place　　　Toys on a table, starting with four then six then eight different small toys

Look　　　At each toy for 5 seconds & then turn around

Tell them　You are going to teach them a fun way to remember their toys

You will be going through different rounds to increase how they remember

Goals for each round:

Remember toy type

Remember toys type & their color

Give each toy a name (Names that rhyme with object work well.)

Remember go slow

Allow different number of toys for each child

Remember names

NOTE: **I know that if you remember five then it messes up the name of Four Memories For Memories**

You'll be amazed & proud of how much they can remember

Example (for the first time use only four toys)

Pick Four small toy animals

Round #1

Pick toys Whale, Rabbit, Bear, Dog

Round #2

Add colors Blue (whale), White (rabbit),

Red (bear) & Brown (dog)

Round #3

Add names Wally Whale, Roy Rabbit, Doug Dog

Round #4

Add both Wally Blue Whale, Roy White Rabbit, Doug Brown Dog

Round #5

Repeat Last to first - Doug Brown Dog, Roy White Rabbit, Wally Blue Whale

VARATION: Use with chores

Round #1

Chore Make Bed, Vacuum, Clean Sink, Fold Clothes

Round #2

Add color Blue Bed, Yellow Vacuum, Silver Sink, Red Clothes

Round #3

Add name Makey Bed, Vicky Vacuum, Sparkelie Sink, Pickemup Clothes

Round #4

Add All three Makey Blue Bed, Vicky Yellow Vacuum, Sparkelie Silver Sink, Pickemup Red Clothes

Round #5

Repeat Last to first Pickemup Red Clothes, Sparkelie Silver Sink, Vicky Yellow Vacuum, Madey Blue Bed

NOTE: **Once FOUR toys & or FOUR chores are easily remembered then add FIVE or more**

Concept Origination

How much can kids remember?

Kids seem to like to name toys they play with. They also seem to like to tell stories about each toy.

What would happen if doing the same thing could be used as a memory learning process? Try it, you'll be more than amazed at the outcome.

NOTE: **Simply be amazed**

*2 By the way, a dog was able to remember over 100 toys by size, color & names. They were also able to learn TWELVE new ones a day.

#75 Music Tales - PB

Every Song tells a Story

Ages   6+

Use   Rainy or indoor days & when playmates are over

Benefits Gives you a break

Materials Kids CDs player & large clock with second hands

Tidbits   Appoint the oldest child to operate the CD player

Play in room or outside

Results   They learn to listen to lyrics & to use their imagination

Design

Pick out Five or six kid CDs before starting the game

Give   The oldest child the responsible for playing music

Give   The youngest has the responsibility of being the timekeeper

(They watch second hand of clock for 60 second time limit)

Parameters Play: CD ONE minute

Tell story: ONE minute

Give   At least each child at least three turns

First two turns:

> You play part of the oldest child
>
> Once they get the hang of it, go take your break
>
> The song leads you into a story
>
> If they get stuck, then they just repeat what the song says
>
> The oldest child picks & plays CD for 60 seconds, then stops the music
>
> (Oldest) makes up the first 2-minute story based on the words of the song
>
> Each child has two minutes to tell his story

After TWO minutes:

> Music starts - the next oldest child gets ready to tell their story
>
> When the song stops - they either continue the first story or create their own
>
> Keep doing turns until song is finished
>
> Repeat with other songs

NOTE: **Each child can ask for the part of song to be played again to help them remember the words before telling story**

> It's very important to support the stories & fun
>
> There are no bad stories

VARATION: Play as musical chairs, as the story goes round & round

> If they can't, continue the story, then they have to sit down until there's only one standing

#76 We're Talking Stockings

Years go by the Memories Remain

Ages	6+
Use	Two weeks prior to Christmas
Benefits	They make something that brings years of memories
Materials	Large pairs of red, blue, green socks, glitter, Elmer's glue & miniature toys
Tidbits	Don't try to be perfect
Results	They will start their own ritual of Christmas fun
Design	
Place	Newspaper under each sock
Write	Their name in glue on sock
Put	Glitter over the glue
Shake	Out excess once it's dry
Glue	Miniature toys, fun stickers, etc. to stockings
	(Everything is allowed, just don't make too crowded)
Hang them	On mantel, etc. as homemade Christmas stockings
	Homemade = lifetime memories
VARATION:	Make a large banner out of red felt material using the same process but with bigger results
Use	The glue to write Christmas phrases & names
Cover	With glitter & toys

Personal Note:

> They will be a family favorite on the wall or
> over the fireplace or years to come

> I created this over THIRTY-FIVE years ago.
> Everyone who made them still uses them for
> Christmas

#77 The "H" Club - PF

There's an "H" in Every Day

Ages	All
Use	As often as you can add it to the day
Benefits	Keep them focused on the good stuff
Materials	Poster or something to view the words often
Tidbits	Think in terms of feel-good words starting with "**H**"
	Share good feelings with another
	Write the words down so you both can see them
	Tell them that they are members of the **"H"** club
	Help them to get at least sixteen "**H**" words
Results	They keep the good
Design	"**H**" club is an activity that reinforces good feelings no matter their age
Create	Words to live by

Example:

Use	The letter "**H**" every day
Start	Your list with the word "**Happy**"
Ask	Them to tell you when they are "**Happy**"
Tell	Them when you are "**Happy**"
Ask	Them to help you create a list of fun words that start with **"H"**
Tell	Them it's a special list just for you both

NOTE: It will be important to tell them the meaning of each word

Post the words in places they can see

Use them as often as you can

Help them notice when they come up or when they hear them from others

Great words for the list:

Honest Hurt Humor Hilarious Hideous

Hot Helpful Harmony Have Handy

Honor Heartfelt Heart Heaven Humorous

Humble Hungry Home Heroic Human

Helpful Healthy Husband & Hug Honest

Concept Origination

Do positive words really make a difference?

It started as a joke but then it snowballed. I'm all about bringing awareness to the good stuff, this works too. They will forever pay attention to all the good words that start with the letter "**H**."

BONUS: HONOR, HAPPINESS, HONESTLY, HOURLY, HOWEVER, it comes it comes from the HEAD or the HEART

Communication Category #4
"Reward"

78 Hooky with Me
Days long remembered

79 Like You
Don't be surprised

80 Feet First
Never let "defeet" get you down

81 Feet Treat **- PF**
If puddles weren't to play in, why would they exist?

82 Simple Simon
Love is all around

83 I'm 8 Years Old Too
Two times is the charm

84 See My World
Come see what I see

85 Get the Point **- PF & PB**
It all adds up

86 Frayed for Fun
Something new from something old

87 Big One, Little One **- PB**
Here for each other

100 Dove Tail - TS
One time for this too

101 Tell Me Now - TS
I'll take the chance

102 Half Birthday - PF
Another reason to celebrate

#78 Hooky with Me

Days long Remembered

Ages   8+

Use   **TWO - THREE** times during the school year, on Fridays or to complete homework

Benefits   Motivates them to get grades within their reach

Materials   Time (Fridays) to take them on agreed upon reward adventure

Tidbits   Sometimes give it to them anyway for real effort

Results   They really try to reach academic goal

Design

Give   Only as a reward activity as a recognition that they're accomplishing something special

Tell them   At three times during the school year, you will be checking their progress

When they reach goals:

Reward them With a **"Hooky with Me"** trip either for an extended weekend

     A trip to their favorite restaurant or whatever is deemed special, etc.

Make   A list of fun rewards

Set   A standard together for success

     Be sure there is absolute understanding of what is expected

Praise them For their good work

Once they reach their goal, make a scroll detailing what they said that they were going to do & what they did in remembrance for the achievement

Example: Hear Ye, Hear Ye by the powers vested in me as parent of ...... & in recognition for the achievement of......

I do hereby acknowledge ......

In consideration for such .... is now the proud participant of the **"Hooky with Me"** gift as follows...........

NOTE: **Something corny like that goes a long way for futures successes**

Tell them This special treat will be repeated

(As long as they live up to their part of the agreements)

When they miss their mark

Talk to them About what they thought caused the problem

What can be done about it before the next opportunity for **"Hooky with Me"**?

Allow them Opportunities to renegotiate their goals

#79 Like You

See the "You" in Them & the "Them" in You

Ages   6 - 9

Use   You want them to feel (even) closer to you

Benefits   Creates a look close to yours (they'll copy you anyway)

Materials   For girls - same outfit including purse & shoes

For boys - jeans, shoes, shirt & hat

Tidbits   See how it goes if fun; try again, if not, once is enough

Results   You in mini form (only occasionally)

Design   This works because your little ones want to wear your clothes, act like you

To show you that they are a **"Big Girl or Boy"** just like mom or dad

Go   A step further let them mirror you in your actions for a day

If too much take them out on a "date" lunch or shopping

Watch   Their delight

Experience them

Being with you as a girlfriend too

It will be fun to watch them be like you, if for only this one time

Concept Origination

Do parents really know that they're heroes?

I remember seeing commercials as a kid of little girls dressing up in mom's clothes or in dad's shirts, etc. You may not be their heroes forever, but if You can be for at least a little while longer, why not take advantage it.

NOTE: **You will be pleasantly surprised how they display their parent heroes**

#80 Feet First

Never Let "Defeet Get You Down"

Ages	6+
Use	Feet hurt or the mood hits you
Benefits	Feet are massaged
	Share a bit of pampering
Materials	Hot warm soapy face cloth, towel & foot lotion
Tidbits	Take your time
Results	Taking care of each other

Design

After washing Their feet

Comfortably sit

Facing them on a couch & extend your legs

Slowly begin

To rub the feet with hand lotion

Don't worry about being like a professional

Gently knead

Their feet (hopefully, it won't be too ticklish)

Enjoy Their tiny toes, soft feet & their happy reactions

Don't be surprised if there are giggles in the beginning or just quiet conversations

NOTE: **This pleasure will be a very sought after ritual when everyone has sore, tired feet**

It will be a natural lesson of how to give & not just receive

(By the time they are eight they will give to you too)

Concept Origination

At what age do you learn to give to others?

No, I don't have a foot fetish, but I have spent many years running. I can relate to a good foot rub. I also like to pamper & be pampered from head to toe. **MWA Kisses** take care of the top - **"Feet Treats"** can take care of the bottom.

This simple caring act will be passed down from one generation to the next.

When was the last time you were rubbed the right way?

NOTE: **It is what JESUS did**

#81 Feet Treat - PF

If Puddles weren't to play in, why would they Exist?

Ages   All

Use   On warm rainy days & just plain hot days

Benefits Shows them how to turn a rainy day into a
              fabulous play day

Materials Sprinkler, large garbage bags for wet clothes,
              change of clothes

              TWO towels for each child

              A plastic sheet for your seats just in case

              (At home) - lots of good hot soup

Tidbits

Let them Change into new clothes when leaving

              Know your park prior in order to reduce
              accidents with rocks, roots, sprinkler heads,
              etc.

              Yes, they will get grass, mud all over them

              They will also laugh a lot & use up all their
              energy

Results   Neither you nor they will ever grow old as long
              as you play in the puddles

Design

Get   Next day's weather report & all the needed
              supplies into the car

Let them Know that they get **"Feet Treat"** tomorrow
              when it rains. (They'll love it!)

As soon as it starts raining get them & head out to nearest park that has shelters

Don't be surprised if you're the only ones there, it makes it even more special

Once you've inspected the park, make sure that they understand to only play where you tell them

Let them   Run around with or without shoes through any puddles

Lead them   (They will think you are the coolest)

Create   A contest as an incentive for them to really splash

After about an hour, they'll be ready to go

Wrap them   In towels, wipe them down, get some soup in them (don't be surprised if a nap is in order)

Believe me, they'll love it; just ask my nephews & nieces!

NOTE: **If there is no rain you can still have almost as much fun playing in homemade puddles**

Your sprinkler at home will work great; they can run through the sprinkler or go buy the original slip & slide or heavy thickness construction plastic.

Concept Origination

For what are puddles really made?

There are very few images in my mind that bring me more joy than the vision of a child splashing in the rain. I wanted mom & dad to be a part of this joy too.

For the sake of a few wet clothes this timeless fun can stay with them for all of their life,

BONUS: You will remember how fun it is to play in a puddle again or for the first time I know, I still play in the puddles.

#82 Simple Simon

Love is All Around

Ages   All

Use   Hmmmmmm, how about ....often!

Benefits   Shows the value of a gift of love

Materials   Heartfelt remembrances

Tidbits   Keep it simple

Use your imagination

Let them know that you think of them

Love them without store bought gifts

Results   More ways to show & to share love

Design   At unexpected times, give your kids something simple that you define as a reminder of love

A key is for you to add your meaning to the items

With your meaning, the items will mean more than just getting another.... toy

Be creative

Examples   Big apple or orange - a colorful rock - favorite type of flower, etc.

Designate a **"Love Chair"** (to snuggle up with you)

Light in their room as-a **"Love Night Light"**

Create a **"Bad News Bear"** to carry when they have to tell you something they really don't want to.

NOTE: **The important thing is to tell them that when you give it to them that it means LOVE from you to them**

Show that you think of them & show your love in a **"Simple Simon"** Way!

#83 I'm 8 Years Old Too - PF

Two Times is the Charm

Ages	8 (could be 9 or 10 – best with older kids)
Use	When you want to check in with them in a unique way
Benefits	Makes sure they feel comfortable with sharing all things
	Stress reliever for you
	Helps you to escape the mad, mad world for awhile
	You remember what it's like to be a kid again
Materials	Whatever they want to play with & video camera comes in handy
Tidbits	Hang in as an 8-year-old for the whole play period
	Do not interrupt play for phone calls, etc.
	If they let you know that they want you more as a mom than a friend, don't get your feelings hurt
Results	You'll learn much about yourself
Design	You are not going to be a parent for a while
	You will be just like an 8-year-old playmate (really do it!)
Pick	A game to play then begin acting just like them
	Don't break the spell (at least for an hour)

After about 10 minutes not only will you get the hang of it, but you will morph in your kids' eyes from parent to a real kid

Hang   In their there's magic here

Talk to them

About anything & even your fears when you were their age

Ask about   Frustrations you might see that they're having but haven't told you of

Use   Simple but probing questions:

Examples: How school is going?

How do you like your teachers?

Who are your friends?

What about boys (girls), likes & dislikes?

Talk   About some of your issues about how a mom feels that they can understand (for instance how mom feels bad when she has to yell at them to do something)

Ask them   What they think would be a better way to get them to act

These honest & free conversations lead to a lifetime of **"Normal & Meaningful Communication"**

NOTE: **Playing 8 years old works great for at least one time**

Concept Origination

Can there be a better way to communicate with children under their terms?

This worked when other ways were not effective.

I've always been intrigued by the fact that we tell friends things we never tell anyone else. With just a few adjustments, I was able to create an environment for little ones to accept me just like they would be a friend. Amazing conversations have resulted between them & the "new" 8-year-old.

NOTE: **Don't be surprised if after only 1 or 2 times of you being eight with them, that they express their desire for you to be a grown-up again. (Oh no, unintended consequences). Once may be enough for you (& them).**

#84 See My World

A chip off, the old block & pictures to prove it!

Ages	4 - 7
Use	Seasonally or when you're curious
Benefits	See life through the eyes of your child for a day
Materials	Digital camera
Tidbits	No rules, it's ok to have a **"few"** off limit places
	Be within ear shot during the day
Results	You'll see their world
Design	**"See My World"** gives you some real insight, laughs & another perspective of living as a (FOUR foot tall) kid again
	They share with you the things that mean to them
Find	Out the things that mean **"little to you"** but means **"a great deal to them"** & the other way around

Encourage them

To take as many pictures as they want of anything that looks: silly, fun, sweet, nice, not nice, etc.

When they're finished go through pictures with them

Have them	Explain what the pictures mean (you'll be enlightened)

Concept Origination

What would it be like to be FOUR feet in a SIX-foot world?

I didn't know, but I realize it wouldn't be hard to find out especially with digital cameras. They could simply point & shoot.

Immediately we all can see what they see, much of which is also pretty funny.

NOTE: **Not so bad way down here or needs some attention**

They may not say can't, but you will realize why something is HARD at FOUR feet tall that is easier at SIX feet tall

#85 Get the Point - PF & PB

Everyone Wins!

Ages	4 - 6
Use	Every few months for ONE - TWO weeks
Benefits	Teaches the value of doing small tasks for rewards
Gives them	A sense of accomplishment
	Rewards at certain point milestones
Materials	Sticky pads - **green**, **blue**, **red** & their own envelope (big enough to hold the slips)
Tidbits	Take away points for bad behavior
Results	Cooperation, improvement on all fronts
Design	
Keep	It simple!
Give them	Points when you want them to do something within their capabilities

Points awarded

If they	Try task green = 5 points
	Do most blue = 10 points
	Do it all alone red = 20 points
Create	A list of tasks that get points & points for each item on list

Point values

Beginner - 5 points:

    Washing hands

    Going potty

    Picking up toys

    Coming to the table for dinner after your first call

Rookie - 10 points:

    Helping clean up

    Putting away shoes

    Placing dirty clothes in the bin

    Doing homework (without a fuss)

Expert - 20 points:

    Making bed

    Brushing teeth

    Get dressed

    Cleaning room

    Once points given

Place Colored slip in their envelope at the head of their bed

    It's very important to give points often & for no reason (it keeps it fun & keeps them interested)

Make Bonus point times (the "when" doesn't have to make sense)

Example Five points: for singing a song

Twenty-five points: for helping bring in the groceries

Help them win!

Give Rewards

Ice cream treat, a walk in the park – go to movies – go out to eat at

their favorite restaurant – go swimming – skating – bowling - to library, just play with them

VARIATION Let them save their points in order to get bigger prizes for tasks done all week (rewards are given at end of week)

Don't worry about perfection encourage them, notice even smallest improvement

Have them Write down their running tally of points as they get them on a chart at the head of their bed.

Remember They can hold their points for a bigger prize

You'll notice their point budgeting techniques to get what they want

NOTE: **It's also very important that you take points away from them when they misbehave (don't be too hard - even if they must learn the bad with the good)**

Concept Origination

Could kids keep themselves motivated at a high level?

The answer was yes, even better than I could ever imagine. **"Get the Point"** uses a combination of energy, a bit of competition & small rewards. The reward itself isn't as important as the challenge.

The points become very important & are cherished. This was another fun way of seeing how their little minds work & what was important to them at their age.

NOTE: **Points can be taken away for bad behavior or stored for bigger prizes when won.**

#86 Frayed for Fun

Something New from Something Old

Ages   8+

Use   Anytime rain or shine

Benefits   Creates fun pair of shorts from old pair of jeans

Something they make

Materials   Old pair of jeans & sewing tool (to pick threads apart)

Tidbits   Yes, you can just buy readymade frayed pants but where's the fun

Talk a lot about anything while working (playing) at it

Help get them started or if they get stuck

Great during long car drives

Can work on anywhere or anytime

Results   They create something that will last all summer

Design

Rough cut   A pair of jeans

Fraying   Pull "**horizontal thread**" down to the end of the leg until soft white threads appear, now something else can be frayed (other than your nerves)

While working on the pants it's a great time for story telling

Conversation topics will come about that may not otherwise arise

Once completed: take picture of them in their creation

For additional creativity: Spray paint frayed part, put sparkles on or anything to make them even more unique

They'll feel **"Real Cool"** & have another memory of creating with you

#87 Big One, Little One - PB

Fun being either "Big" or "Little" (Sibling)

Ages   7+ (to be the **"Big"**)

Use   When **Little"** needs help

Benefits   Teaches **"Big"** brother or sister to help **"Little"** **"Big"** learns responsibility **"Big"** & **"Little"** learn to help & to be helped

Materials   A "**Task**" & "**Taught**" Checklist (w/Gold Stars)

Tidbits   Explain what it means to be **"Big"**

                 Designate **"Big Time"** to be responsible

                 Give times for **"Big"** to teach **"Little"**

                 "Big" gets help from parents

Results   **"Big"** & **"Little"** are proud of what they achieve

Design

Create   A chart separated into columns:

Task Learned, Task Taught

Put   What you want them to do in **"Task"**

                 Tasks **"Big"** learns from in **"Task Learned"**

                 "Big" gets a Red Star in **"Task Learned"**

                 When **"Big"** teaches **"Little"** put in **"Task Taught"**

                 "Big" gets a Gold Star in **"Taught"**

Example: Task Learned Task Taught

Tied Shoes Red Star Gold Star

Dress alone Red Star Gold Star

Set weekly or monthly goals of tasks to accomplish once reached

Give them   Praise, rewards, your time & hug me treats

NOTE: **If "Big" gets stuck he can ask parents' help**

Concept Origination

How could I help siblings bond earlier so that it would last a lifetime?

I've always heard about resentment between siblings. Resentment seems to be very common, especially when there were a few extra years between siblings. This resentment seems to be unnecessary. Instead of avoiding the obvious, I decided to make it an asset.

I thought it to be good to let each sibling learn the wonderment of each other's importance in the family. By doing this, they would quickly begin to share much more together.

They would soon begin to help each other when they knew that that was what was expected of them. I saw so much great interaction between my girlfriend's girls that I couldn't resist making it a positive addition. I even coached them to work with each other more often.

BONUS: Friends can come from different ages too

#88 Sanctuary - PB

Begin their dreams, Express their dreams & their dreams will come true on the walls

Ages   All

Use   Anytime & Often

Benefits   Gives you a break

Provides a sanctuary for each person

Keeps you in touch with what a child is doing

Materials   Small paint brush, various color paints, soft marker & poster boards

Tidbits   Anything goes in this room

Can be played alone or with the whole family

Doodling encouraged

Protect the floors

Paint directly on walls or poster boards

Note: **Be sure to take a picture of it each year**

Results   Their growth & maturation is expressed all the time

Design

Designate   A spare room or wall to become **"Sanctuary"**

Put   **"Sanctuary"** sign on the door or in the room

Limit   The amount of furniture or clutter to two chairs, floor lamp so that nothing can be hurt & to maximize space to create

Make   Projects for the whole family

If someone wants to create by themselves simply put a signup sheet on the door

Why (creative expressions):

- To grow creativity in all forms

What?

- Any type of art, drawings, words, sentences

Where?

- Anywhere in the room, even the ceiling

When?

- A set night to read & to explore new additions

Notes: **It's not about how good something looks It's about creating & doing!**

Walls must be able to be painted over

All project materials stay in the **"Sanctuary."**

Part of the fun is not worrying about this room

Monthly   Everyone explains their work

Yearly   Family repaints room

Start again Soon you'll wonder why it took so long to have this magical place

NOTE: **If something comes up on the walls that concerns you, ask them what it means, then discuss**

Concept Origination

Shouldn't everyone have a place to be themselves?

Should everyone have a place to feel safe?

I originally thought of this idea from watching a movie over forty years ago. In this movie, it seemed that every time the main character had a problem, he would see his older friend. Every time he visited his friend, the friend was repainting his living room.

While the friend painted, they both talked about the problems. It seemed strange but in reality, it was therapy for both & it worked for both.

I liked the fact that the room changed as he needed it to. The room was a safe place for both of them to communicate.

By having a sanctuary, you could keep up with what's going on at any given time with them while having a creative outlet too.

NOTE: **A sanctuary ahhhhh is just nice**

#89 I'm Big

They'll be "Big" when you let them be "Big"

Ages   6+

Use   You want to teach them one or more than one task together

Benefits   Makes sure they can actually do the task & creates self-reliance

Materials   Patience in the beginning till they get confidence

Tidbits   Your encouragement is a must

They will naturally want to be treated like a **"Big"** kid they'll ask for more complex tasks

Results   They will be & act **"Big"** making your life a bit easier

Design

Give them   Tasks that only a **"Big"** kid wants & can do

Put   Task out there as a small challenge

Challenges = chores (initially)

Picking out & putting on their own clothes

Washing or taking a bath by themselves

NOTE: **They will really want to finish it with your encouragement, praising & reaffirming that they are "Big"**

Concept Origination

Could recognizing kids as **"Big"** help both parent & kids?

Kids always say it & hate it when they're not recognized. I wanted to recognize & encourage them to "be."

It never ceases to amaze me the age at which little ones want to prove that they can have more responsibility for themselves. Letting them be **"Big"** encourages them by using simple reverse psychology. For instance, if you want them to make their bed, challenge them by saying; You know… a **"Big Boy"** (or Girl) could make their bed. Are you a **"Big Boy"** (or Girl)?

It works as long as you just nudge them (don't push).

NOTE: **The little ones will be big enough soon, don't miss this time**

#90 May Day Play Day – PF

More than a play day in May

Ages	4 - 8
Use	On a May Day or a week before Memorial Day Weekend
Benefits	Everyone participates & it builds confidence
Materials	FOUR kids+
	ONE to SIX parents (one parent for every three kids)
	Water hose (sprinkler too)
	Volleyball set
	Frisbees
	Kick ball, something for bases
	Jump ropes
	Large pillowcases (or burlap sacks)
	Cloth strips for Three-legged race
	Large spoons, plastic or real eggs
	Whiff-a-ball set
	Large beach ball (TWO or THREE)
	Picnic food or just snacks
	Lots to drink
	Sunscreen

Tidbits	Everybody plays
	Throw off your fears of not being good enough as everyone is good enough
	Do it for them – they'll love you for it
	Keep each activity under a half hour
	(Unless they are having a fantastic time then make in an hour)
	Be flexible - goal is not how many activities they play but how much fun
	Expand to June, July & /or August
Results	Everyone wins - everyone has fun
	Brings your kids, playmates, parents & you together for a great day of play
Design	This takes some planning & coordination (well worth the time & effort!)
	TWO or THREE weeks out contact your kid's friend's parents
	Each parent is responsible for bringing one item to play with
Meet	At a local park or large backyard
	Everyone brings food but the main attraction is the fun activities that they get to play together
	Each parent participates a station
Setup team	Each team to at least THREE kids & ONE adult
	The more teams the better

Men can participate, women keep score or reversed

At least FOUR games: half before eating & half after eating

Volleyball (lower the net) for smaller kids

Three-legged sack races (pillowcases) (at least FOUR teams – team = TWO kids or kid & adult)

Wiffle ball set (SEVEN to TEN per team)

Kickball or dodge ball (at least SIX people per team)

Frisbee toss course

VARIANCE - Once everyone gets the hang of the activities have a time for a FOUR kid team against a TWO-person adult team

After the activities & the meal

Give special prizes for whatever categories you think of.

Create   Activities that bring out different strengths of each child, something for tall kids, shorter ones, etc

Concept Origination

Does anybody really have to grow up?

One of my most favorite days while I was in elementary school

"MAY DAY PLAY DAY"! I made a slight variation by bringing in the neighbors & friends together.

Everyone has a part to play; everyone joins in young, old & even older. What could be better than food, fun & friends of all ages?

NOTE: **If you can find Red, Blue & White ribbons then use them for FIRST, SECOND & THIRD place. Red ribbon for first place gives them twenty points, Blue is second place worth 10 points & White could equal third place for 5 points**

#91 Discovery Shopping - PF

Learning on "YOUR" terms

Ages 6+

Use Spur of the moment without spending a lot of $

For school projects

For finding play wear

Benefits Teaches them how to make choices

They will learn:

The value of money

Their dollar limits up front

To make choices

It really doesn't have to be new

To budget: Do I pay for a used item, or do I save my money for new?

To bargain: Would you take less?

Materials Go to out of the way consignment shops, garage sales, Goodwill stores to buy fun used clothes, toys, etc

Tidbits Limit amount of spending of $5 per item or up to $20

Find locations within ten miles of home

Results Have fun & inexpensive shopping adventures

You will no longer be the bad guy saying "no"

There will also be far fewer tantrums

You can say "yes" more often

You discover a lot about them & you

Design   When kids say they want it, need it, my friends have it, or I've got to have it

The type of purchases that are forgotten soon after purchasing

Have a fun while teaching a lesson without breaking the bank

You will be amazed how much fun you can have for so little money

Concept Origination

Do moms deserve to do what they like to do even with their kids?

How can you give moms time to enjoy their shopping fun, while having kids along with them? The answer: teach them how to shop with you.

Teach them in a way that there would be virtually no conflict the whole time. Without them fighting etc. mom could get more of what she liked without the headaches or stress.

NOTE: **You must do it so you might as well have fun**

#92 Pre Pet

That they must really take care of a best friend

Ages   6+

Use   When they are pushing for a pet

To determine if they can take care of "their" pet

To teach them what it will really take to have a pet

Benefits   All of you will know when the right time is to have the **"Real thing"**

The correct time will show itself

Materials   Book of dog breeds to familiarize yourself with health issues & temperament of different breeds

Bigger stuffed animal

Animal care items

Water bowl

Pet food

Leash

Brush

Tidbits   Take it slow in the beginning

Become more vigilant as the period goes on

Learn what it means to take care of a pet

Continue project for at least a week (preferably more)

Results   Pet will be taken care of by "them"

Design   As a big step in teaching what it means to have a pet

Have   Frank talks about what it means to have an animal

Tell them   That they will have to treat their pre-pet as good as a real pet before they can actually get a real one

Create   A schedule that they have to stick to for: walking, feeding, brushing & keeping the water full, for their stuffed animal just like it was a real one

Have them go with you

Buy   All the animal care items needed for a real pet

First few days

Do everything with them

FIRST week

Have them do the work & then check on them

If they waiver or stop helping

Revisit in 3 to 6 months

SECOND week

See if they do the work automatically

If they get it, keep going for 2 more weeks

THIRD week

Discuss the differences between a stuffed animal & a real animal

Beginning FOURTH week

Take them to a shelter to look at dogs

Make An agreement with them about what you & the pet expects of them:

It'd their responsibilities (not yours)

Agree On a Six-month trial bases (but be prepared to keep the pet regardless)

Get them The pet – allow for THREE or FOUR visits before deciding

Keep them On their routine

Help them But don't let them give up their end of the bargain

NOTE: **They will now understand& that pets need their love as much as they need the pet**

FUN FACT: When I was a volunteer at a no kill dog shelter many times the pet actually picked the new owner. Be ready to really notice how the pet responds to your kids

#93 Paint Me Please - PF

**Great painters all start somewhere
why not here…. Why not now?**

Ages	Whole family & neighbors
Use	Sunny days or winter/rainy days indoors (garage)
Benefits	Creativity explored without the worry about getting dirty
Materials	Each child wears a large, collared button-down white shirt (pants must be ok if paint gets on them
	Canvas drop cloth
	Paint brushes at least an inch wide
	Metal pie dish pan to hold each child's paint
	EIGHT to TEN Different latex paints
	CD player & kids' songs approximately TWO minutes in length
Tidbits	Supervise for the paint
	Each child has one color
	Mae sure shirts are completely dry before taking them off
Results	**"Paint Me Please"** shirts become favorite play wear
Design	
Put	About a quarter of a tube of color into each child's pan before they start

"Rules"   Paint only on the t-shirt & above the belly (no faces)

Everyone gets painted

Everyone stays outside until shirts 100% dry

At no time do they paint anything but shirts!

Play TWO songs during each paint time

Only you can give more paint

You paint too

Help them   With the first two shirts

Then you can keep playing or leave them to their own creativity

All the painters circle around first **"Paint Me Please Kid"**

There is only ONE **PMPK** at a time

Everyone else has a brush & is a **"Painter"**

Everyone gets a turn in the middle to get painted

After you give everyone paint & they get some on their bushes

Start playing

A song

PMPK continually turns around slowly for two minutes

"Painters" brush **PMPK's** shirt as **PMPK** turns

Everyone stops painting as soon as the first

#94 Kid Creation

Genius is right here

Ages	6+
Use	Anytime
Benefits	They create without concern for the "Kid Creation" being good enough
Materials	Toys & tons of stuff that are already in the house
Tidbits	Ask a lot of questions
Example:	Oh, really & how big was it?
Results	They learn confidence
Design	
Let them	Be the activity master & creator
	You become an easy-going playmate
	No need for this to make sense to you
	No need for there to be a winner or a loser
	If a winner is needed, give in only at the end
Allow	Yourself to let go
Enjoy	The pleasure of playing with them
Put	All kinds of "stuff" on the floor
	They create an activity using what's on the floor
Ask	lots & lots of questions
	How?

PAINT ME PLEASE

What?

Where?

When? (They'll fill in the blanks)

Go   With the flow

NOTE: **Each time you play something new will be created**

You'll be amazed with what they assemble the **"stuff"** & how they use it

Concept Origination

When does confidence begin?

I'm always amazed at what goes through a little one's mind. Instead of just letting things happen or ignoring them, I wondered what would happen if they were encouraged to take the reins all by themselves? I know & you will too. They never run out of ideas.

NOTE: **Don't waste anyone's mind, nurture it**

#95 Kids Rule - PF

Build confidence one day at a time

Ages	5+
Use	Best on weekends
Benefits	Gives them control for a few hours
Materials	Their imagination & your fun spirit
Tidbits	Play along no matter how nonsensical the activity seems
	Give them this opportunity as a treat
Results	They take on responsibility
Design	Kids decide activities for the day away from the house
Give them	Guidelines: time, distance, etc.
	Once there, it is up to them to take the lead
Give up	As much control as possible
Keep	Reinforcing how much fun their choices are
	If they get stuck, give them some suggestions
NOTE:	**TWO children or more, use "Helpers" to work together**

They need to feel like they are making all the choices, praise them for their effort use it as a **"Get the Point"** reward

They make the choices of:

Where to play or where to eat

What movie to see, etc.

No matter what comes out of it, it is important to praise them for their effort

Oh yes, just for fun you can act like a brat if you like (They may recognize that character)

#96 Colorful Days - PF

Now a "blue" day is a fun day

Ages   All

Use   You pick it

Benefits   Gives them something to look forward to

Materials   Large monthly calendar

Tidbits   Guide them but let them choose

Results   You'll learn a lot about their needs & wants

Design

Choose   A color for each type of event

Mark   "In or out" (for inside or outside)

Frequency   A few days

A whole week

A whole month

Event time from half hour to entire afternoon

Try   To follow each day but have some flexibility

There can be more than ONE event per day

Outdoor events:

"**Park It**," "**Little Campers**," "**Paint Me Please**"

Indoor events:

"**Pillow Talk**," "**Clean Up**," "**What's Cooking**"?

Pink event:

Something with Mom

Blue event:

Something with Dad

White event:

"Family Matters," "Dove Tail," "Shelve It"

Orange event:

Eat out, movies, amusement

Red event: Travel

Once event is decided, fill in the calendar date

You pick Some of the events

Make Sure that they have a voice for a few of the dates

Concept Origination

If we see the good days, do the bad days go away faster?

I'm a visual person. I believe that if you see & make time for both the "fun" & the "must do" activities there will be much less conflicts or upsets. By using a big calendar, the fun & must do choices can be made & seen on a day to any basis.

After just a brief time of charting the type of activities, there were fewer phrases like "I never get to" or "I never have any fun." All the "choices" are clearly marked for all to see in living color.

NOTE: **Color each day brightly**

#97 What I Like

Let nature take its course

Ages   6+

Use   To encourage their individuality & to develop their confidence

Benefits   You see what is "natural" to them

Materials   Pictures of activities

Tidbits   This is not always easy to encourage & help them to be who they "naturally" are instead of what you would want them to be

The rewards are much longer lasting for them & for you

Notice the subjects that they learn quickly

Subjects they show special interest in or talk about

Don't force what you'd **"like to see"**

Pay attention to what **"actually appears"**

Look for signs of **"unhealthy stress"**

Expose them to different music, dance & athletic programs with you, family or your friends within & outside of your own interests

It's really about their future not yours

Your little ones will quickly realize the difference in someone who is really in love with what they do

Share your creative passions too

Results They (& you) will be happier by spending time on the natural strengths instead of forcing the unnatural

Design Fun for you is to enjoy the process of finding your children's natural talents

As their talents are discovered you will both have more fun doing what is natural

They'll quickly exp& their abilities with your encouragement

It's up to you to pay attention

In beginning, it may be hard not to force your desires on them

Overall everything will work out so much better for you & them if you focus on their natural tendencies

Look At those you know who love what they do for a living

Identify Others who really enjoy what they do (they're everywhere)

Give them A call

Ask them How did they discover their calling? When did they notice it?

How were they encouraged? etc.

Then bring

Your 7+ year old to have a talk with them

Sometimes it's those we're close to & sometimes it's total strangers that impact a child's life, use both worlds for your kids benefit

I'm amazed how many people that I know who found what they wanted from the age of 7 or 8.

Is that you too?

As soon as they begin to show a **"natural affinity"**

Ask them   What do you like & why?

Being indoors or outdoors?

Playing on a team?

Performing on stage? Etc.

Encourage them

To ask to do the activities they like the most

They'll quickly take you up on the offer

Many activities may become a dead-end but don't give up

They will love the fact that you are paying attention – to them & their **"natural wants"** & **"tendencies"**

NOTE: **Some possible future dream careers can originate right from home like**

Crafts - "We're Talking Stockings, Cooking - "Kitchen Wonders,"

Dancing - "All Shook UP," Singing - Performance Plus"

Encourage, Recognize enjoy & watch them blossom

Talk   About progress to them as often as you can

NOTE: **If you are still hesitant about taking this step – go to the library & read some biographies of some of your famous heroes – read how they started their trek**

Just imagine

If some of them did not go down their natural path what the world would have missed

Remember Being aware & then go with what is natural will help you to spend your time & money in the right places with help & encouragement, they may never have to work a day in their lives!

NOTE: **Sometimes dramatic events cause a person's direction in life. That may be ok but wouldn't you rather the direction came from joy, fun or passion?**

#98 Park It - PF

Can you see what I see?

Ages All

Use Sunny days are great

Benefits Great way to go to the park

Materials Adult **"Helper"**

Whistle (for you)

TWELVE small flags attached to wires (find in hardware store)

Place them beside **"Adventure Items"**

At least SIX kids & one helper mom

Six 4 X 6 Note pads

THREE Pieces of Three-foot rope to hold on to

Large poster board & black marker

"Home Base" where mom sits with poster board within the middle of boundary

Small awards for each category (be creative)

Tidbits

Work In pairs **"Big" with "Little"** & make **"Home Base"** in center of boundaries

Results They learn to really look at things

Design Helper goes ahead of group makes a list TWELVE **"adventure items"** to find

Examples: #1 Red flower

#2 Pinecone

#3 Tree trunk

#4 Big rock

#5 Wooden fence

#6 Swing set, etc.

Mark   Everything in a circular pattern with view of **"Home Base"** (In the center of the boundary)

Number   All items from ONE to TWELVE on poster

Number   Each flag corresponds to an item. Use the flags to mark off each of the TWELVE adventure item

Anchor   Each flag beside each "adventure item"

Give   **"Adventurers"** writing pad

Tell them   On the top of the first page of their pad to write these three questions to answer about each item

What color am I?

Am I alive?

Do I feel hard soft?

To find any four items

Write   Number of flag & items name

Answer   All three questions

Then to come back to home base

Answers don't really matter

It's just a chance to learn how they think & observe

Give an example:

Item # 1 - A leaf on a tree

Hints: #1 I am green

#2 I am alive

#3 I am soft

Rules They can't go out of the boundaries

They must work as a team

Each pair must hold to piece of rope as they search & not let go

There's a Ten-minute time limit

They must answer the THREE questions for each item

As soon as they find FOUR items, they come back to home base

Ask If there are any questions

Tell them They will get a prize at the end for 1 of 6 categories:

(No need to take too seriously, just an excuse for each to be good at something)

Laughing the most

Running the fastest

Being the loudest

Finishing first

Having the most fun

Giving the best description

If SIX kids, each should win one category, more kids = more categories

Watch them

Round one Blow whistle to begin search

Stop after 10 minutes

Ask them IF they have any questions or need help to finish writing

Let them Finish writing before going to next round

NOTE: **It's not the most important thing to find all four but to keep the energy up, they will get better each time you do it**

Round two

Blow the whistle to find the second category of 4 (see round1)

Round three

Repeat for the last 4 (see round 1)

When finished

Have them

Sit in a circle around you at home base

Read What they wrote

Give Awards

Concept Origination

Can you really see things in more than one way?

I always define a great city by its parks. There are more ways than just the typical ways of using a park. What would going to the park be like if all five senses were really used while there? I created many different park activities, all five senses, I know & now they know.

NOTE: **Count all the parks in your county or city & visit each one**

#99 Keep it Quiet - PF & PB

Silence really is golden

Ages	6+
Use	When a nap is necessary for you
Benefits	They play & you rest
Materials	Your original direction
Tidbits	Keep them in the same room
	Your role: keep your eyes closed for FIFTEEN minutes
	Your partners help
	You might want to play **60 SECOND SCREAM** first before doing **the Keep it Quiet**
	Quiet type of activity
Results	AHHHH - FIFTEEN minutes of rest you didn't have before
Design	Kid-proof everything
Lock	The doors
	Your partner
Explain	To them the fun will be to play without any noise or just whispering (whispering or being silent is the activity)
	You'll be surprised how well they'll do it
Practice	One of them plays your role
	You play their role

Place   Homemade **"quiet area"** sign around the area to be quiet

Make   An agreement: No sounds where the signs are

Give them Prizes at the end of your break

NOTE: **Set an alarm for yourself just in case you get too comfortable**

Concept Origination

Could I get kids to buy into being quiet is fun?

They do get it & play their **"quiet parts"** extremely well to give mom a restful break.

BONUS: You learn what quiet really is

#100 Dove Tail - TS

There's a time for everything

Ages	8+
Use	When they are giving you grief while giving them an option
Benefits	They learn to make decisions
	Take responsibility for completing task later
	Relieve the stress of trying to complete something now
Tidbits	**Dove Tail** defined: Delaying completion of task for 2 days - no exceptions
	Limit frequency of use
	Pick time to complete the task & stick to it
Results	They do chores without grief
Design	
Ask them	To do a chore
They tell	You that they do not want to do it now
Stop	The urge to argue
Tell them	They can use **"Dove Tail"** to do it later
	When they agree they sign a piece of paper with chore
	Write **"Dove Tail"** & the date of completion
	You sign then put on their bedroom door
	Then, forget it until the time comes

NOTE: **There can be no complaining when the time comes regardless of whether they have to give up fun to finish the "Dove Tailed" chore**

Once completed

They give you the paper back

You will be pleasantly surprised how often they would rather do the chore instead of using their **"Dove Tail"**

Give them TWO **"Dove Tails"** per week to use

#101Tell Me Now - TS

When "now" is the time

Ages	6+
Use	When **"Dove Tail"** is not a good choice
Benefits	Teaches them to take a chance & the value of doing it now
Materials	Trust
Tidbits	Be spontaneous & flexible
Results	They get an immediate answer
Design	Kids take a chance & make a request of you
	When they don't want to **"Shelve It"** they can ask you to **"Tell Me Now"**
	It lets you immediately say yes or no without any grief from them
Don't think	Too much
Give	In more than you normally would
Feel	What it's like
Make	A snap - **"YES"**
	Compared to - **"Normal Parental NO" to the fun of a snap, yes** ("NO" for not a good reason)

#102 Half Birthday - PF

Half as good is good too

(Dedicated to my oldest brother Dennis born on December 25th)

Ages	All
Use	Halfway through their birth year
Benefits	Just a reason to have fun & celebrate also they'll love it
Materials	Your fun spirit & half a day (of course)
Tidbits	Stick to it **"Halfway"** use half a cake, half a party
	Homemade presents – all in **"Half Fashion"**
Results	New **"Family Tradition"** is born
Design	
Give them	A special celebration day (SIX months past the original birthday date)
Just do	It with **"Half the Effort"**
Ham	It up
Talk	About it Invite half as many kids over
Have	Half a cake, etc.
Example:	My birthday is October 5; therefore my half birthday is April 5
NOTE:	**"Half Birthday" will become a special day because you declare it to be!**
	You both will feel great about it!
	They will also love the fact that no one else celebrates **"Half Birthdays"**

PERSONAL NOTE:

> **"Half Birthdays" are especially great for kids who were born on holidays. My brother, was born on Christmas, never got a birthday party just for him with "Half Birthdays" celebration, he does now**
>
> For birthdays that fall on holidays:
>
> Celebrate Holiday Kid's **"Half Birthdays"** like their real birthday
>
> While their real birthday as a **"Half Birthdays'**

Example We celebrate my brother's **"Half Birthdays"** on Christmas

> We celebrate "Full" birthday on his "**Half Birthday** date" June 25th
>
> **"Half Birthdays"** are a good excuse for fun, they really love it

Concept Origination

> What if you were born on a holiday?
>
> My brother Dennis never had a real birthday party because he was born on Christmas. I decided to help all those children born on holiday & to give all others another chance for a celebration.

NOTE: **Being half is special too (ask any 85-and-a-half-year-old)**

PERSONAL NOTE: I know people who were born on New Years Eve, New Years Day, Christmas, July 4th to recognize a few. To a person, they couldn't celebrate their birthdays without the holiday taking over. They love HALF BIRTHDAYS now.

This is the END OF PART ONE.

Continue to a sneak preview of PART TWO of I WASN'T Kidding, NOW, I AM the next one hundred ways to increase confidence for FOUR- to TEN-year-olds

Part 2 A Personal Parenting Tool Input Request

Thank you again for purchasing "I Wasn't Kidding, Now, I Am." I am proud of the many positive comments that I have received. These comments come from parents who have used some, most or all of the **102 different tools** to truly connect with their kids.

Drop me an email with your parent tool (s). I'd love to hear about your favorites & the results.

I realize my examples are only the tip of the ice burg. Moms & dads from all over the world creates unique & effective ways of connecting with their kids.

Please **send me a one-page** description of ways you've connected in your family to accomplish the basic objectives of this book: to **Build their Confidence, Develop Creativity, Enhance Communication, Increase Bonding, Provide Loving Discipline & Saving You Time.** Include your name & phone number.

You may be called for further clarification & receive credit in the book. From these submissions I will compile –

I Wasn't Kidding, Now, I Am
The next one hundred ways to increase confidence for FOUR- to TEN-year-olds

Part 2

If your activity is chosen, I will send you the first version in eBook format at no charge, as a thank you.

Please visit my website **www.FamiyConnectionsforLife.com** to read more ways of getting the Relationships You Dream of & deserve. Get what you want or get back what was lost with parents, siblings, friends, etc.

To be added to the email list in order to be informed of "I Wasn't **Kidding,** Now, I Am **Part 2" release & other products from ………email me at**

Rory@FamilyConnectionsforlife.com.

NOTE: Your email will not be shared with any other entity

Something about children is so unique & special, I had to write about a moment

I Wasn't Kidding, Now, I Am

Older & Wiser Kid Confidence Builders

Part 2 – Sneak Preview

Copyright 2023

103 Music Appreciation

Hear again for the first time

Ages	7+ (two to four)
Duration	Fifteen minutes up to an hour
Uses	To help children to appreciate the value of music in movies & when there is no music
Benefits	Children listen to the changes & meanings of music in movies
Materials	Three different age-appropriate movies
	DVD or TVOE to play movies
	At least three notepads & pencils or pens
Tidbits	Children often hear music in movies but don't consciously relate music to actions or emotions
	Learn to separate music out of movie to better appreciate it
Results	**"Littles" & "Bigs"** will be able to understand the meaning of movies by the mood being

established & supported by different kinds of music

Will understand how to use music to change their own moods

They will understand the **why** of changing moods & the **how** to pick music to change their moods, the how

Children may decide to play instruments or to sing to change their & others moods

A greater number of music genres will be appreciated & recognized

Design

Pre-Watch Three movie segments (3 to 5 minutes each or as long as song is) that they already know (ie., Jungle Book, Frozen, Dumbo)

Examples of simple music

AT the beginning of movie during credits

During excited time (car chase for example)

Emotional time (sad or happy for example)

Rescue or hero times

At the end of the movie

Note scenes on notepad & time of each

Also notice music in commercials (15 to 60 seconds)

"Littles" & "Bigs" close their eyes & describe what music is supporting (help them with what & why)

Have   Two up to four Little & Bigs play at the same time

Ask   Questions & tell them to raise their hands to be called on to explain their experience or mood for each music segment. (no wrong answers just have them explain why)

After each has answered

Have them   Open their eyes & discuss their answers now that they are watching. Any different feelings when watching? Explain

Concept Origination

I'll have to give the credit to Mrs. Lee (my second-grade teacher). She made me aware of how much music impacts movies. Without it we were left with much fewer interesting movies

104 Listening Hard is Easy

New, New & New

Ages	8+ (two Bigs)
Duration	Five to Fifteen minutes
Use	To enhance listening skills
	Gain better understanding & increase attention span
Materials	Short story, age-appropriate books or articles
	Stories they know all about
	Stories they know nothing about
Tidbits	Patience is needed
	Reward for good results
Design	Everyone is settled down & quiet the first time through
	Two Teammates tell 2 **Bigs** (8 – 10) that they will show them how to listen & to understand what is read to them
	Two calm teammates - One reads to the other then asks questions while **Little & Big** just watch – each read about a minute long
	No one interrupts or makes any noise
	Then **Teammates** gets up & gets loud for three minutes to get pumped up

While still pumped up & repeat reading of **teammates** (overcome distraction of being pumped up)

Then **Teammate** reads to one of the **calm Bigs** then asks questions of each about story

Calm Big reads to the other big then asks questions – **Teammates** monitor & help

Then **Bigs** get up & get loud for three minutes

Once done get ready to repeat reading & questions of **Big to Big**.

Comment on how different when distracted & when not

NOTE: **Keep reading & subject short & easy in the beginning then increase length of readings**

Reward good results with favorite fruit

Concept Origination

Another elementary teacher gave me this gift. My fifth-grade teacher Mrs. Gore (English Estates Elementary Seminole county, Florida). She said to practice difficult listening. She also said to focus on the message instead of the messenger. It has helped me throughout my entire life.

NOTE: **I can get something out of anything said whether or not I like it or agree with the subject matter.**

105 Two Minute Too Clean

No Decay, I Say

Ages	**5 – 7 (one – three Littles)**
Duration	**Two minutes per little one**
Use	**Daily**
Benefits	Less trips to the Dentist
	Foundation is made for a lifetime of results
Materials	Phone stopwatch
	Toothbrush for each
	Toothpaste
	Teammate
	Wash cloth
Results	They learn & take practice for themselves
	Less cavities
	Less fear of Dentists
Tidbits	Reward with favorite activity from
	Part ONE I Wasn't Kidding, Now, I Am
	Let them time you also
Results	They would automatically like to add time until they reach desired two-minute goal

Design   Best in the morning but also night before bed

Have **"Big" helping "Little"**

Teammate puts toothpaste on each toothbrush (not too much)

Teammate says to brush each of sixteen **"teeth areas"** brush five strokes each – for a total of eighty strokes

Let **"Big"** use timer on Teammate

Teeth areas

#1 Top left (flat area of top teeth)

#2 Top right (flat area of top teeth)

#3 Bottom Left (flat area of bottom teeth)

#4 Bottom Right (flat area of bottom teeth)

#5 Inside bottom left of teeth

#6 Inside bottom of right of teeth

#7 Inside top left of teeth

#8 Inside top right of teeth

#9 Outside of top right of teeth

#10 Outside of top left of teeth

#11 Outside of bottom of left of teeth

#12 Outside of bottom of right of teeth

#13 Front top left of teeth

#14 Front top right of teeth

#15 Front of bottom of left of teeth

#16 Front of bottom of right of teeth

Have **"Bigs" touch each area** of teeth described above

"Bigs" Brush one thru sixteen of teeth areas

Teammate times and counts to five for each area

Teammate repeats doing ten **strokes (back & forth equal one stroke)**

"Bigs," time **teammate** for **at least one minute**

Switch **Teammate counts** to **ten strokes** for each area **until all sixteen areas are brushed**

Teammate times **"Bigs" (goal is two minutes)**

At the end of two minutes have **"Bigs"** run their tongues over teeth to feel how smooth that they are

Use wash cloth to clean up any sink mess

NOTE: **Let them do an activity from Part 1 (for day)**

Let them do wind down music (for night) for about half an hour before bedtime for about 15 minutes (It begins a routine for sleep too)

Concept Origination

This originated from a show & tell in the fifth grade. A dental assistant told our class to brush each of our teeth ten times. From that time on, I have always counted to myself.

NOTE: **I can report that I have never had a single cavity**

I Wasn't Kidding, Now, I AM

INDEX/GLOSSARY OF TERMS: THESE ARE VERY IMPORTANT & FUN

6

A

B

D

E

F

G

H

I

L

M

N

T

W

Y

About The Author:

Rory Hill has spent most of his life as a salesperson. A salesperson who listens & who has always been interested in others, especially kids. As a salesman who would leave a client better off than he found them. He earned customers' trust & then turned them into lifelong repeat clients. **He has been using many of these times tested "tools" for over 35 years.** His dream is to leave a legacy that honors parents while cherishing the next generations. He now lives in Boynton Beach Florida with his girlfriend JoAnn & THIRTEEN-year-old Shitzu named Bitsy. No kids but Six nephews & nieces & EIGHT great nephews & nieces & hundreds of little ones he has worked with in reading programs for kids between the ages of FIVE & TEN.

CREDITS:

*1 Nordquist Richard

An introductory literary nonfiction thoughtco. Aug 26, 2020, Thoughtsco.com/what is literary nonfiction – 19133

*2 Daily Wire October 6, 2021

*Love From a Child   *11/22/06*

Inspired by little seven-year-old named Kylie
By Rory Hill Copyright 11/06

Today, I was given the precious love from a child
Nothing so natural, nothing so pure
Nothing can touch me more; nothing can touch me the same
Today, I was noticed by the closest thing to God, an
innocent child

Nothing was given with such ease yet with more meaning
Nothing was given more freely
This pure love, perhaps only to be given at no other time in
their life
Knowing love with or without our adult & sometimes tainted
leaning

There's nothing like the love from a child
The only thing that comes close is a kiss from an angel
A kiss sent from God, maybe they're the same thing
It only comes when they decide as well

A child as innocent as a messenger from God, honest & free
This love is a never-ending gift straight from Heaven
Nothing can compare to the beauty from He or she
They are untouched by the prejudice or pains yet given

When they look out from their eyes, they see only, the good
They know what is real & what is not in their space
They share with others, especially with those others who
would also
No matter of looks, status or race, they give but only from
their space

They have a heart totally filled to share
They know deep inside who really cares
If you're lucky, they will take you by the hand too
They always begin by sharing with their tiny smiles that
shines thru

How could anyone deny their special love?
Although they are little, they spread their big love with smiles
& laughter
These are mixed with sounds of screeches & howls forever
after
I often wonder why such purity fades like the flight to above

How could anyone deny their special love?
Although they are little, they spread their big love with smiles
& laughter
These are mixed with sounds of screeches & howls forever
after
I often wonder why such purity fades like the flight to above

How could anyone deny their special love?
Although they are little, they spread their big love with smiles
& laughter
These are mixed with sounds of screeches & howls forever
after
I often wonder why such purity fades like the flight to above

I do
I have received love from little ones many ways so & many
times
From black, white, boys & girls they all shared their love
They have the freedom & wisdom that only God too
possesses like the white dove

So, for now, sleep little ones
Today was a big day full of surprises, wonders & magic
Tomorrow, I promise more of the same kind of funs
Sleep, oh little ones, I will protect you now without any kind
of trick

I will protect you from evil & ugly times
Times that may make you hard
Times that may make you hold back
Times that will eventually take you away never to come back

Grow if you must
But never lose your heart of love
Never lose that trust in good, rainbows or magic
Never stop sharing all of the special you

Your hands are so small
Voices so tiny, eyes so bright
Soon you will be like me
But like you, I will never forget the times, I too was free

I will never forget the love you gave so easily
I hold on to it tightly
I give it back to you at the time of your need
I will never fade in my joy of you rightly

You were made from love
You were born of love
The perfect gift as God could ever give to any
Keep the glow in your heart for many

I will be there for you
Thank you for your love
May you also receive the same from your own children
someday
May you too have a child made with this kind of love & joy, in
their heyday